Editor: Jeremy Tunstall

The silent watchdog

In the same series

DAVID MURPHY

The silent watchdog

The press in local politics

CONSTABLE
London

Published in Great Britain 1976
by Constable and Company Ltd
10 Orange Street London WC2H 7EG
Hardback ISBN 0 09 460920 9
Paperback ISBN 0 09 460930 6

Copyright © 1976 by David Murphy

Set in Monotype Times
Printed in Great Britain by The Anchor Press Ltd
and bound by Wm Brendon & Son Ltd
both of Tiptree, Essex

'The dog did nothing in the night time.'
'That was the curious incident,' remarked Sherlock Holmes.

Sir Arthur Conan Doyle, Silver Blaze

Acknowledgement

The research for this book was financed by the Social Science Research Council.

Contents

PART ONE

The silent watchdog

1
Introduction

It is generally an unspoken assumption in discussion about the press in Great Britain and in the United States that it is in some sense a bastion of freedom, a safeguard against the various assaults which are made on democracy. The 1962 Royal Commission on the Press, for instance, seemed to equate free economic competition among newspaper publishers with a 'free press', linking it in some undefined way with the 'public interest'. The public interest – a concept of philosophical dubiety, but which many establishment figures turn to in their hour of need – was not defined by the Royal Commission, and it remains unclear what precisely the Commission meant by a 'free press'. What does seem to be demonstrable on the basis of the evidence which is to be examined here, however, is that at the local level at least, where governments cover up except on rare occasions, the press does not uncover, cannot uncover and has no inclination to uncover.

Justification for the free press usually relies more or less implicitly on the notion that as an institution it fulfils two functions: that it provides a forum for ideas and a source of accurate information on which the public can base wise political judgements. The contention here is that much that is vital to enlighten judgement about government is not revealed by the press, and it is not revealed in the first place because of a number of legal constraints and organizational characteristics – both of government and the press – and in the second because of perceptions of events by the journalists involved. One aim of this book is to show by reference to a number of case studies the kind of procedures by which governments cover up and the kind of pressures, almost always indirect, complex and not necessarily intended, which inhibit journalists from investigation.

Despite the apparent parochialism of the local press as a subject of study, it is frequently at this level that news stories involving issues of individual political rights and the malfunctioning of the basic components of the democratic system have their genesis. On many occasions these stories do not see the light of day or are disregarded over a period of years until the pressure of events brings issues to light in a non-journalistic context: the bankruptcy court; a government tribunal. What we are concerned with then is why some stories are not published and others are, and the sociological and political circumstances which form the context of these outcomes.

There are broadly two kinds of story in which we are interested: those involving simply the observation and recording of overt political and governmental events; and those in which there is a conflict between the governed and various agencies of government. In the latter cases typically it is the governed who are out for maximum publicity and exposure in the interests of some form of change in government policy, while the government agencies seek to minimize public revelation of their activities – for a variety of reasons. Let us look then in general outline at the coverage of local news which is available to the citizenry of this country and at the reasons for its taking the often abject form that it does.

There are in general five channels of local news coverage available in the large urban centres of Great Britain. From the most parochial to the most general these are: the local weekly paper; the local daily paper (usually only an evening one although some provincial mornings survive); local broadcasting; regional broadcasting; and the national press. An important element in this context is the local freelance news agency, especially in determining what news item qualifies as a good story, because this is often the source by which news media at city, regional and national levels are alerted to stories of general interest at the borough or parish level. The chief concern here is with the press, although broadcasting features to a considerable extent in one of these case studies.

The local weekly press makes a poor showing as an object of study. At the mention of the parochial names of the local newspapers looks of amused contempt leap to the faces of academics engaged upon, say, studies of criminality among the Watutsi, or the educational backgrounds of flagellant nuns in southern Italy. This is hardly surprising. No one who has been involved in local newspapers can have escaped noticing that many people regard them as unsophisticated, parochial and overfull of births, deaths and marriage announcements, not to mention advertisements for second-hand paraphernalia. But despite its limitations, the weekly newspaper in Britain performs a key role in the news-gathering network. In this it differs radically from its counterparts in the United States. This key role serves two main functions: the provision of trained personnel and trade-union members, and the supplying of news both as tip-offs and as written-up news stories to other parts of the news network.

It has been noted by the Royal Commission and elsewhere that the local weeklies act as a valuable training-ground for young journalists, who later move on to evening papers, Fleet Street and broadcasting. The Commission also noted (as the National Union of Journalists has complained over the years) that in this the weeklies shoulder more than their share of the burden to the benefit of Fleet

Street. Perhaps this criticism by the NUJ is not entirely fair, since one of the reasons for numerous young local weekly reporters joining the union is that NUJ membership is a precondition for working on the bigger papers, and opens up channels of promotion. For instance, the young reporter hears through his union branch of vacancies on larger papers and of opportunities for part-time work in national offices – which is one of the ways leading eventually to Fleet Street. And frequently the local weekly office provides pasture for an old Fleet Street workhorse who may be a survivor of the *News Chronicle*, *The Sketch* or *The Graphic*, or simply a victim of drink or hardened arteries. In this way the journalistic trade acquires a sense of unity which doubtless leads to the high rate of union membership and relatively high level of militancy for a white-collar union.

In Manchester, where the national dailies and the Sundays have regional offices, the weekly men form a significant element. They act as night subs, night-duty reporters on the national dailies, as subs, reporters, photographers on the Sundays, and do holiday relief work in the summer. Undoubtedly management uses the knowledge gained of their potential both as journalists and organization men when making permanent appointments. Moreover, such part-time work supplements the otherwise relatively meagre income of the local journalist to a level approaching equality with his daily colleague. This and the fact that he is engaged at least for part of the time on the same kind of work underpins his sense of belonging to a relatively homogeneous trade. Of course, this situation is more common in the areas around large urban centres than in the provincial hinterlands. But at even the most parochial level journalists make contact through freelance work and union membership with colleagues and management on local evening papers, and even with the regional and national press.

In the rural and smaller urban areas this absorption of the weekly, bi-weekly or small evening newspaper into the national news network takes a number of forms. The journalists on a small-town weekly may be the accredited freelances to whom news editors turn when they want routine court, council or inquest coverage in the area. Usually in the event of something like a contentious strike or a murder the nationals will send their own 'fire-brigade' reporters and photographers. This of course varies from newspaper to newspaper. The *Daily Telegraph*, for instance, carries wide coverage of local news, which is similarly obtained from freelance correspondents while a paper like the *Daily Mirror* is only interested in local news inasmuch as it is gossipy, snappy, sexy, shocking or whimsical. But it does rely on material being sent in and has a network of correspondents throughout the country.

Basically there are four kinds of relationships between the free-lance reporter and the national and regional dailies. He may be a correspondent or a freelance on a retainer, in which case he may be called on by the paper in advance for coverage which he then owes to the paper; he may be an accredited freelance, in which case the NUJ protects his interests in the event of usurpation by an outsider in the coverage of routine matters for newspapers and the Press Association: or he may send in work on a casual basis, simply spotting a 'good story' and selling it as best he can. The fourth relationship is one initiated by the national newspaper when a staff reporter, who may be drumming up interest in a circulation drive, goes to local newspaper offices for contacts with the local community. In some offices such men are established callers who bear gifts from the petty cash and stand rounds of drinks in return for infor-mation. In others, where evidently they threaten the local hegemony of the weekly reporters, they are asked bluntly to leave the vicinity.

Local news which is reported in the national press may be of great importance or may be simply sensational: the dealings of Mr Poulson for example, or the Moors murders. On the other hand it may be frivolous but eye-catching, on the lines 'Widower remarries first wife whom he divorced in 1933' (he is pictured with twelve children, twenty grand-children and two corgis). 'You're never too old to fall in love, even for the second time', says blind one-legged Bill, a seventy-three-year-old lion-tamer from Market Harborough. Often the local press – through the processes suggested above, is the means by which events are selected as being appropriate for consider-ation as national or regional newspaper stories. There appear to be two factors influencing this process of selection: the organization of news-gathering and publication and the perceptions of the news-gatherers and writers. Let us examine these briefly.

The weekly newspaper office attracts news and it finds news. Because it is at once a newspaper office and also local, small-scale, approachable, it is a lodestar for a variety of local axe-grinders, egomaniacs, paranoids. Its polished mahogany, inlaid lino, glass panels and dust conjure old ladies reporting men stealing electricity in their lofts, Jehovah's Witnesses giving advance notice of Arma-geddon, opponents of water fluoridation – international big business palming off the by-products of the aluminium industry for profit – drunks complaining about the smelly conditions of the gents in the pub next door, an irate lady with a broken heel asking, 'Why your paper doesn't do a story about the hole in the path outside my house'. Among these divers voices crying in the wilderness are bearers of more quotidian tidings, sons returned from fortune-seek-ing, a proud father announcing his wife's delivery of triplets or the approach of his daughter's nuptuals. These form the bread-and-butter coverage of the local weekly. Some of those who provide it may be established news contacts who produce good tips on occasion. A regular visitor to one office was a garrulous lollipop-man who used to come in for a chat about his invented experiences in Hollywood in the 1930s, but who also knew all the gossip in the local Conservative association and gave the paper first crack at a scandal which continued to be covered in the national and regional press for several months.

What is distilled from these contacts as useful is written up, or in the case of advance notice of events such as weddings or spring fairs, entered in the office diary for coverage. Information is also telephoned and written in by contacts – headmasters, vicars, local government officers, officials of voluntary organizations and political parties. These contacts have often been carefully trained by the newspaper over a period of years into coming forward with news, and recognize what will make news.

The office diary is the means whereby the editor knows what needs to be covered and who is covering it: it contains appointments to see golden wedding couples for 'pic' and interview, the place and times of inquests, court cases, royal visits, strike meetings and the opening ceremony for the new sewage works. Against each job the initials of the reporter and photographer responsible will be entered. The newspaper's coverage of such matters as councils, courts, inquiries, tribunals or inquests is routine and is directly or indirectly protected by the legal obligations of such bodies to execute transactions in public view. Ceremonials such as mayoral dinners, the opening of exhibitions, the inauguration of a new commissioner of boy scouts are routine coverage. The participants want the publicity and the editor needs the news material, especially accompanying pictures with seas of full faces to boost circulation.

In all this the newspaper is totally passive, waiting for news to come in. But the paper also looks for news. Reporters make daily, weekly, monthly or occasional calls on a variety of contacts. These contacts occupy two kinds of position: officials who are 'gatekeepers' in some formal network, or they are unofficial, local barrack-room lawyers, leather-mouths, receptacles of secrets who are nodally placed in informal neighbourhood, family or workplace networks of gossip. The daily calls are made to the police, fire and ambulance stations, hospitals and the coroner's office. They may be by phone or in person. The personal visit is most likely to be made at the police station. The call may be a highly formal inquiry to an office holder, or it may be a friendly chat with a particular policeman or hospital secretary whom the journalist has known over a number of years. The information gleaned may be directly related to official business, details of accidents, fires and deaths, or it may be news of police wrestling tournaments, hospital dances or personal anecdotes about a fireman who has built a yacht in his back garden.

The weekly calls are made on people who are known as good sources of information, those well disposed towards the press. One paper may as a matter of policy send its reporters around to all its newsagents in an attempt to set up a network of informants. The general intention is to get news from all the geographically separate parts of the circulation area. The reporter visits or phones vicars, mayors' attendants, shopkeepers, social club secretaries, trade-union officials and company PROs. Less frequent calls are likely to be made to headmasters, librarians and choral society secretaries, whose flow of information is geared to longer time periods such as school terms or seasons.

There are two further important sources of news-gathering. First, there is the inside knowledge of a community to which a reporter or editor has access by virtue of living or working in it. A friend who teaches in a local school may tell him that children are eating in a school hall which has been condemned by building inspectors but whose findings have been suppressed. The local MP has quietly divorced his wife in London to avoid publicity, it is rumoured in the Labour Club. An alderman's wife has been charged with soliciting and robbery out of town, so the gossip in the Old Victoria Hotel runs. Second, there is the information which is acquired by the newspaper office as a by-product of other activities. Advertisements often contain a news item: unusual business activities being started, new job opportunities in declining areas and so on. Reporters and photographers on assignments such as mayoral initiations often pick up news stories from a town-hall superintendent or some functionary's chauffeur.

What happens to the news once it reaches the newspaper office? There are four dominating constraints in such an office: time, space, money and circulation. They do not all pull in the same direction, however. For instance in a competitive situation where a paper is fighting for readers, all the emphasis will be on the widest and most up-to-date coverage of events. This demands the ability to alter pages up to the last minute. It also demands a large journalistic staff and means maximizing the editorial content of the paper. All this involves additional expenditure of money and space, for not only are they costly items in themselves, but they impinge on valuable advertising space. And what these constraints have in common is a tendency to emasculate the local press in the role in which it sometimes poses – that of the independent, investigating watchdog of democracy. With the perceptions and values of the journalists involved, especially those of the editors, these constraints bring about a situation in which all the advantages lie in producing news that depends on the mimimum amount of research and digging and all the disadvantages in news that may be informative but is troublesome in its gathering and in its consequences: namely that which requires skilled investigation to find, clarify and substantiate, and which is sufficiently threatening to powerful individuals to provoke them into vengeance.

In examining how these processes of conformism affect a newspaper it becomes apparent that the journalist's own perceptions often reinforce the effect of external constraints. These internalized limitations on his part derive from a combination of local values, which he has imbibed through living and working in the area, and his preconceived views as to what constitutes a good story – which he has acquired through his contacts with his co-professionals. Of course this is not to deny that many journalists do not willingly accept these values or the external constraints on them.

When the local newspaper editor comes to create his edition for the week or the evening he has to assess: (a) the raw material – bits of information – in the light of how much space he has available, which is calculated on the basis of a ratio of news to advertisements, the advertisements being a controlling factor; (b) the cost of particular kinds of coverage; (c) the circulation pull of any particular coverage, bearing in mind the audience to which it will be directed; (d) the need to have something in the paper by the deadline, which is at the same time up-to-date. The reporter is aware when collecting his data of these sorts of factors, because he is acquainted with the news editor's or editor's previous responses to similar material.

This creates a situation in which the ideal type of story is one which involves the minimum amount of investigation – preferably a single interview – or the redrafting of a public relations handout, which can be written quickly and cut from the end backwards towards the beginning without making it senseless. It must also have the strongest possible readership pull. This is the minimum-cost, maximum-utility news story. In the *Sun* it expresses itself in its most extreme and mindless form – the bum-tit saga: 'Here's a lovely girl with two big problems on her mind'. . . . In the local weekly it is the sad parade of detailed, lurid court cases which enable the paper to deal in violence, theft and immorality, completely protected from libel so long as the court reporter's shorthand is good, and at the simple expense of sitting a reporter in a court whose events can be summarized according to predetermined formulae.

Let us look at the sort of story which does not get published and the sort of angle which does not get used, and examine the reasons why not. First, there is a class of story which is tackled only by the underground press, *Private Eye* and, sometimes, the *Sunday Times* 'Insight' team. This takes the form of an investigation of allegations of governmental corruption. The reasons editors and reporters give for avoiding this kind of subject are the cost in terms of manpower and the dangers of libel action. They do not acknowledge being afraid of antagonizing local leaders, but this does seem to have an indirect influence upon them, a factor which will be examined later. Secondly, there are stories which ridicule the whole process of local government. The reason frequently put forward by journalists for their reticence concerning these is kindness towards councillors. Thirdly, are the stories which would give the background to council decisions and make plain the kind of political considerations which lies at the root of such decisions. Editors usually explain this in terms of the lack of interest on the part of their readers.

Let us look at these types of story in terms of the different types of local news coverage which exist, beginning with the weeklies. Weeklies are usually either chain newspapers or owned by a single family. In either case they are likely to have staffs of around half a dozen reporters, which on the face of it would seem inadequate for a close scrutiny of council affairs. However, since these reporters have usually been based in one locality for a number of years, they are well aware of the scandals, background to decisions and the ridiculous aspects of the governmental system which nonetheless appears in the news they write up as columns as a serious well-run affair. As to the family newspaper, the proprietor is likely to belong to the same social class as those who are politically and economically influential in the area, while the editor is often committed to the paper and the area for his livelihood and status. In the chain newspaper the pressure is more subtle. The editor must always show a profit; if he fails to do so, the centralized managerial department will want to know why. He will therefore aim to expand circulation and keep down costs. Above all he will try to avoid risks. Twenty-five boy scouts pictured leaving for a trip to Switzerland should sell twenty-five papers without controversy. On the other hand while a story revealing an inefficient town-hall department may sell extra papers, it will probably cause news sources in the town hall to dry up, and council members or their friends may cease advertising. Playing safe by sticking to straightforward stories avoids this sort of trouble. Even if circulation falls and profits melt away after the editor has imposed a 'responsible régime' on his newspaper, he will probably survive in the organization. In a situation of stringency no one wishes to be marked out as a troublemaker – in such a state of affairs, a further fall in profitability might well have direct consequences.

These tendencies are more marked where there is competition between two papers. In this classic situation, outlined so succinctly by the Royal Commission, one paper almost inevitably goes to the wall. They fight for survival by minimizing costs, and at the same time attempting to brighten up their presentation. For instance, when I was a junior reporter on a local weekly, the competing paper put back its publication time so that it 'went to bed' about two and a half hours after its rival. Thus on Wednesday afternoons one of its reporters would search our paper for any stories they had not covered and then rewrite or paraphrase them, ensuring for no extra cost that they had every story they wanted in our paper plus their own 'scoops'. For such papers the costs of one libel case would sink them without trace. Although the constraints are economic, and the bureaucrats in the newspaper organization usually leave editorial decisions to journalists, the effect of economic stringency on journalists is editorial constraint. To take two examples:

A number of house-owners applied to a rates tribunal for reductions in rates in a northern town because of the degenerate industrial area in which their houses had been built. They annexed the local paper's reporter at the hearing and told her that their complaint was against the builder – a prominent local figure who, they alleged, had sold them the houses without letting them know the true nature of the site. They had moved into the area from a large conurbation. The reporter wrote up the story, but the editor refused to use it for fear of reprisals from the builder. In another case a reporter found out that a private builder had built an estate on land which the council had turned down as unstable and as a result a number of houses were cracking. The editor would not use the story because he said it might depress the value of other houses on the estate and the owners might sue the paper for damages.

Internalized constraints in terms of the editor's absorption of local perceptions and values are equally potent. When looking at the working methods of an independent weekly I accompanied a reporter to a rates tribunal which heard three cases. One involved the reduction of rates because a view had been changed by the building of a factory since the house was purchased from the builder. The second involved a claim for a reduction because of the detriment to amenities caused by noise and traffic from a local transport firm whose yard was behind the house, while the third claimant's grounds for bringing a case were that what had been a quiet passage at the side of his house had been churned up by a local building firm which was putting up houses on a site behind his house, and breaking kerbstones and pavements in the process. All three were given reductions. In the first case the chairman of the rates tribunal was the builder of the house involved; in the second he was the owner of the transport contracting firm; and in the third case his was the firm building the estate. No mention of these facts was made in the reports of the cases, the editor explained the omission by commenting that everyone already knew the extent of the chairman's local business interests.

Squatters in a northern town moved into an area of large Victorian houses that were to be demolished to make way for private flats which the locals did not want. The local council was expected to make a clearance order, which meant that the owner would demolish the houses but retain the land and the council would rehouse the tenants. This would enable the owner to get rid of unwanted tenants at the council's expense while reaping the benefit of vastly increased land values consequent upon the change in use of the land. The land, it should be noted, had been bought up for the property development company over a number of years by a local estate agent and son of a late Conservative councillor, who had also been an estate agent. The company had had a number of different names over a period of years and appears to have been a purely speculative venture whose assets were property bought with money borrowed from a bank. A local newspaper reporter covered the story but was unable to get it published – his news editor saying he would only use it in the event of the squatters achieving their object of housing a fatherless family. As it was, the reporter published in a Manchester 'underground' paper of which he was co-publisher. At a less sinister level newspapers cover up the bumbling confusion which often characterizes council meetings. Councillors' English is improved so that councillors do not appear in print contradicting themselves and mouthing malapropisms. Councillors sometimes get into appalling difficulties over procedure and officials forget papers.

A further pressure on journalists in the bigger evening papers is the need to make a regional appeal and to eschew parochialism. Large evenings or the regional office of a paper like *The Guardian* in Manchester cover wide areas with few men. The *Daily Telegraph* covers local municipal affairs in much detail, but as already noted it relies heavily for this coverage on freelance copy. In Manchester for instance it retains a local news agency. Such organizations sell copy in order to survive: they are interested in the minimum cost, maximum-utility story *par excellence* – work on a story must be justified by income otherwise the agency ceases to exist. Speed, accuracy, reliability and the selection of 'good stories' make for a good freelance livelihood. Digging up news which is unpalatable is difficult, time-consuming work; dressing up an easily available talk by introducing a good angle brings home the bacon.

The notion of the good angle or the good story is vital to an understanding of how both the regular staff of a paper and freelance journalists are sensitized to events. This is a notion of the market in an industry geared to entertaining and titillating. A number of themes can turn an event into a so-called 'good story': novelty, topicality, drama, deferential fantasies, conflict. Novelty can take a number of forms. It can simply be a totally new sort of event: 'Bishop's wife is first woman rugger referee'. Or it can be an inversion of a normal event: 'Spinster rapes skinhead'; or a jocular anecdote – a champagne bottle fails to break at a ship's launching. Topicality is a mechanism whereby the values about events imposed by the media men actually take on a reality of their own. For instance several novelty stories – of sailing around the world or unpowered flight – are sold, and then tales of such activities become topical simply because they are like other stories which have been given credence already. When as a consultant metallurgist Professor Derry suggested that BMC transverse-engine cars might have been prone to steering failure, any journalist who was attending an inquest involving a lurching Mini or 1100 knew he would be able to sell the story to the nationals – even though Professor Derry subsequently withdrew his suggestion about the proneness of the cars' steering joints to metal fatigue. Drama for its part involves suspense, death, violence, sentimentality, sexual deviance of a gross nature, large sums of money – Chunnel to cost £850 million shock report. Deferential fantasies also confer topicality – couples who marry on the same day as royalty, a child being christened on the same day as a royal baby with the same name, a football star's double who claims he is mistaken for the great man. They are a rich vein for the imaginative newsman: they play on a mixture of grovelling servility towards the landed aristocracy and royals and resentful envy of the arrivistes, and are made up of tales of loose living by well-known figures, pools wins transporting hospital porters and postmen's widows to fortune, and the comings and goings of royalty. Conflict is more than simply another form of drama. The best type of conflict, especially for a local paper, is one which will generate 'talking-point' stories – that is, those which will engage the imagination of the majority of readers: 'Should the borough go comprehensive?' 'Should council flats go to unmarried student mothers?' The army collection for Princess Anne's wedding present became a 'good story' when the MP Willie Hamilton expressed public opposition to it. Obviously a story combining novelty, drama, deferential fantasy, conflict and topicality is what the market-conscious journalist seeks: 'Duke of Edinburgh feared lost in midget submarine on underwater round-the-world race. Why should taxpayer pay for rescue, asks Labour MP.'

The basic motivation behind the good story is allied to that of the freelance journalist trying to sell copy. It is the market-orientated view of news and the survival of the newspaper which underly day-to-day coverage of affairs either by staff or, like the *Telegraph*, by freelances retained on a permanent basis. When a reporter has got his information and decided how strong it is in terms of how it measures up to being a good story – a decision which is implicit and unspoken – he proceeds to write up according to a formula. This depends of course on the kind of information he has and how he has got it. In fact the sources he uses are frequently taken very much on trust. When writing up council minutes, for instance, reporters either simply convert the local authority gobbledygook into journalistic form, or alternatively do so with the addition of one or two interviews with officials or councillors. When there is a conflict between one group and another the approach is to get a statement from both sides: an accusation and a reply. For instance an allegation that, say, a council is secretly planning to redevelop an area with more car parks and offices than acknowledged in its official plan, by means of widespread demolition of houses, would be dealt with by publishing a statement by the protest group spokesman together with a reply by the council spokesman. In this way the newspaper satisfies the protesters without upsetting unduly the local authority. At the same time the story probably costs no more than two or three telephone calls or mileage for a couple of short journeys. Getting the initial information, following up with interviews and writing are all likely to be accomplished in less than a full working day – probably within a morning or an afternoon. In other words the story complies with all the organizational requirements of a newspaper working in a market situation. In the case of the evening paper the undertaking runs to daily deadlines; the weekly journalist has to produce several stories a day to justify his hire.

The alternative would be to spend a deal of time looking for evidence, prying into the local authority's offices and into the background of the protesters' allegation. This prying and checking could put up the backs of all concerned, since it would be taken as a sign of distrust. It would also mean that a reporter might be involved in investigative work for days, and with no guarantee of any results. The 'opportunity cost' would amount to ten non-contentious stories.

In summary, there are a variety of factors – especially the pressures of the market and competitiveness which lead towards bland and superficial journalism. There is, too, a contradiction between the 'free press' as an institution guaranteeing the free exchange of ideas and accurate information in a democratic system and a 'free press' in the sense of a newspaper industry which, like any other capitalist industry, sells its goods in competition with others. In the following chapters this contradiction will be examined in the light of actual social processes.

2
The silent watchdog

In order to understand the background to the case studies in the following chapters, it is necessary to examine briefly the history of the relationship between the press and local government; the claim by the newspaper proprietors' organizations, the Guild of British Newspaper Editors and the National Union of Journalists, to be the watchdog of democracy; and the kind of coverage which characterizes the local press as well as the establishment critique of these processes.

In their long struggle with the local authorities to gain the right to cover meetings, the representatives of the newspaper world put forward the following arguments for admission to committee meetings and an overall 'opening up' of public business:

(a) That it is in the public interest that decisions made behind closed doors should be made public through the press.
(b) The earlier stages of council decision-making should be made public so that the public can participate.
(c) The public has the right to know the views of its representatives on all issues.

They pursued these arguments through their representatives, through 'journalists' MPs' in Parliament (eminent among whom was Mrs Margaret Thatcher) and by making representations to the 1947 Royal Commission on the Press. The local authorities' associations resisted extensions to press coverage by every means open to them through the Commission, Whitehall and Westminster. Individual councils flouted the spirit of the law which compelled them to hold full council meetings in public except for specifically confidential issues, by going into committee. It was the 1960 Public Bodies (Admission to Meetings) Act that had laid it down that these full council meetings should not be held privately.

There is little doubt as to the reasons for the resistance by the local authorities to public scrutiny. Both in their speech and in their actions the local authorities manifested a love of secrecy verging on furtiveness. Even five years ago it may have been possible to regard this purely as an example of bureaucratic paternalism. In the more recent light of disclosures concerning the Poulson affair and the weekly trickle of crookery revealed in the pages of *Private Eye*, there is no doubt that at least some local authority officials regard councils as their private businesses whose operation may vary from innocuous amateurism to that of organizations suggestive of a municipal Mafiosa.

The opponents of more extensive press coverage offered a number of arguments against greater public exposure of their affairs. One of their frequent arguments has been that revelations of personal details in, for instance, welfare housing cases or in the matter of individual council employees' salaries, could be acutely embarrassing. Since the rates for jobs as dustmen, bus-drivers, schoolteachers or district nurses are publicly available and in any event would be of no news interest, one can only assume that this argument was designed to protect from embarrassment such blushing violets as town clerks, borough engineers, borough treasurers and city managers. Why should they be embarrassed? Why should the public not know what they are paying public employees out of the rates? As for the individual welfare cases, this difficulty can be overcome by the use of initials in the committee minutes: reporters are not interested in the rent arrears of deserted wives, or the financial circumstances of a handicapped person requiring special assistance.

Their arguments went further: that some councillors would be constricted from speaking freely in open committee; that some would play to the gallery and that these would steal the publicity at the expense of the more serious-minded 'committee man'. Observe that these arguments basically refer to psychological states or personality failings of councillors, not to shortcomings of the press. The further argument of the local authority representatives was that the appearance of recommendations of committees in the press in advance of council meetings might give the impression that decisions had been taken when in fact they had not. In other words, the public should only know when the decision is taken – when it is too late for interested parties to lodge a protest.

Other arguments have included the notion that admitting the press to committees with delegated powers, the purpose of which was to speed up council business, would be administratively difficult. Or that introducing the press might bring the party whips into the committees. In effect the spokesmen for the councils have accentuated the fascist values of efficiency, speed, certainty, consensus. Anything which might involve the public recognition of conflict of interests has to be placed behind closed doors. The fear which has been expressed is that somehow the presence of the press would generate sensation-seeking or histrionic behaviour by councillors, that the impression of a virgin consensus would be sullied by harsh press reports of conflict and disagreement (which the more naïve may have regarded as essential elements of democracy).

A further argument occasionally put forward by the representatives of local democracy is that somehow public knowledge of proposals to buy up land for council schemes would enable property speculators to make profits at the expense of the community. Quite how this would follow is a mystery. If such proposals were made public, it is more likely that property developers would be frustrated from any attempts to cash in on inside knowledge by buying land for redevelopment. The simple reason being that the owners, knowing the score, would not sell. Further, legislation could take account of this eventuality – by the nationalizing of development land, for instance. In any event, prosecutions over the past ten years – in the Yorkshire area, for example – suggest that the present furtive system gives a distinct advantage to property speculators with inside knowledge and that these speculators are often the councillors or officials themselves.

Since the 1960 'Thatcher Act' councils have shown varying degrees of willingness in admitting the press into council and committee meetings. In the local government sphere, the act guaranteed the public and the journalist the right to attend council meetings, education committees and divisional education executives, parish meetings and meetings of public bodies, generally, other than those of police authorities, entitled to levy a rate. The exception to this, as already mentioned, was when councils passed the 'secrecy motion', by which the press and the public were excluded 'because of the confidential nature about to be discussed'. This provision appears to be open to a number of different interpretations. For example, in the mid 1960s, Urmston Urban District Council, a small local authority in the Manchester conurbation, excluded the press when it discussed the reasons for the failure of the central area redevelopment scheme that had been farmed out to a company of developers which had run short of funds and were proposing to reduce the scheme from fifty-seven to thirty-eight shopping units. The company was asking the council to take over extra space in the scheme as offices and wanted Lancashire County Council to take up leases for office space as a branch library in order to save the scheme. There were fairly wide gaps round the doors of the council chamber and it was easy for reporters to hear councillors putting forward the view that if the council did not do what the company asked, it would be faced with a half-completed derelict site which would have to be abandoned. The council complied with the company's request. It was hard to conceive any other reason for the secrecy motion than an intention to hide from the electors the mess that had resulted from an over-ambitious scheme, although the chairman of the development committee had stressed that he could see no reason for going into secret session.

Some authorities have shown an open response and admitted the press to all committees, while others have been able virtually to ignore the act by removing one or two members from committees of the whole council and then continuing to hold their effective meetings in private, retaining the council as a rubber-stamp operation. In 1967, the Maud Committee on Local Government reported that of 715 local authorities of all types, 10 per cent admitted the press to all main committees, 40 per cent to some and 50 per cent to none.

Attendance at meetings and exclusion because of the 'secrecy motion', however, are probably less serious impediments to effective reporting than the availability of documents. The 1949 Royal Commission on the Press report showed that 50 per cent of the local authorities surveyed applied an embargo in documents.[1] The 'Thatcher Act' requires the local authorities to provide a copy of the agendas along with such further information as would be necessary to indicate the nature of business to be dealt with in secret. However, the same clause also provides that copies of reports or other documents supplied to members need only be supplied 'if thought fit by the council'. The Maud Committee again reported that 37 per cent of local authorities still embargoed comment by the press on their minutes and 16 per cent of local authorities did not make their agendas available at least one clear day before the council meeting.[2]

How much legal power then does the press have for insisting on its 'rights' to cover local government affairs? The answer appears to be rather little. The 'Thatcher Act' relies heavily on the good nature of local authorities to implement the spirit as well as the letter of the act. Committees can be closed to the public, the council can operate the device of removal of one member and then go into committee. Or it can pass the secrecy motion. Further, it can control the flow of documents to newspapers, restricting it to bare agendas and the council epitome which, in the case of Manchester Corporation for instance, is a miracle of non-communication. If for any reason the newspaper is truculent, it can be 'punished' by restrictions on news sources, denial of advertisements, or by even being barred from the municipal library reading-rooms.

Nor should one necessarily conclude that the new system of local government heralds a new attitude to the press on the part of local politicians. The Greater Manchester Council has a register of councillors' interests, but it will not be made public. This decision was taken over a Labour motion calling for the publication of the register which, in view of its voluntary nature, offers no guarantee of 'clean' government.

To understand the nature of the external constraints on the local press, it is necessary to add to its impoverished predicament, vis-à-vis its access to local government meetings and documents, its precarious position in relation to the law of libel. The law does not provide a clear protection for the journalist acting in what he regards as the public interest. The absolute privilege accorded to parliamentary and legal coverage is not extended to local government affairs. Not only is this privilege limited if malice is proved, but also if a paper fails to publish adequate letters or statements of explanation. Furthermore, whether particular words or sets of words may be taken as being malicious or libellous is usually open to doubt and sometimes appears capricious. To comprehend the effect of the law of libel on newspapers, it is essential to look at newspaper organization in relation to the sorts of demand which legal criteria of acceptability impose. This will be discussed shortly.

There is certainly nothing in the legal position of the British local press which leads one to a 'fourth estate' view of its predicament. No role as an essential guardian of democracy is enshrined for it in the constitution, nor even in the quasi-constitutional legislation governing British public administration. Unlike his American counterpart who enjoys a traditional legendary role as a democratic institution, albeit rarely achieved in reality, the British journalist is frequently revealed by the opinion polls, not to mention the general antagonism he meets in his job, as a man held low in public esteem. It is as if he is still the faintly disreputable penny-a-line, foot-loose, drunken freelance not too concerned about the truth, selling what he can to whoever will buy it, as he was thought to be a hundred or so years ago.

If this is the situation the local newspapers face, how do they meet it? What effect do the legal uncertainties and constraints have on them?

In the nineteenth century, the local weekly newspaper was likely to be a politically committed, vitriolic, polemical sheet, peddling scurrilous gossip about its political opponents and untrammelled by the law. Whig and Tory booksellers and printers alike would set up papers to lambaste one another's politics. News was only relevant in as much as it fed a picture of an opponent as a first-class scoundrel or if it showed one's own party as blameless benefactors. The journalist's role in this predicament was that of a mercenary dogsbody: his task was not to dig for the truth but to blow up rumour, to catch the ale-house gossip, or if necessary, to invent. He was a sort of literary Liddy or Hunt.

With the stamp-duty reform, the spread of education, the reform of local government and of the Libel Law, the newspapers could aim at wider audiences with a hope of profit, but at the same time had to guard against prosecution for scurrilous libels. The politically 'independent' newspapers at local level flourished often in immoderate and savage competition. Some of the verbal assaults by com-

peting newspapers on one another were worthy of the previous
political battles. But their overt aims were generally to disavow
the disreputable image with which the journalist had been landed,
to offer unbiased coverage of local news in order that their readers
might judge matters for themselves. Leading articles would speak up
for what was right, and not simply for what any particular political
party might stand for locally. Perhaps the essence of the 'new' local
newspaper of the latter half of the nineteenth century was expressed
in the first editorial of the infant *Congleton Chronicle* which denied
sectional and party interests and pledged the worthy newspaper
to impartiality in the interests of what was best for Congleton. In
a sense the new commercial papers of the late nineteenth century
identified themselves with a sort of parish-pump patriotism, a
supra-factional, local, public interest: the same public interest in
whose name they have conducted their battle for greater press
coverage of local affairs.

Despite their localism, the papers were aimed at a 'mass' audience.
They provided all manner of content from stirring adventure or
romantic novelettes in serial form to household tips, shipping and
national news, moral homilies, nature notes, agricultural prices,
as well as the hard-core local news, with the inevitable births, deaths
and marriages. Their prosperity depended on reaching large
numbers of readers and attracting advertisements. In order to
attract advertisements the paper had to be acceptable to the business
community. But since the paper itself was run as a business this
was anyway likely to be the case. The newspaper left the political
arena and, to paraphrase Marx, moved into the market-place; and
in so doing, developed an ideology of impartiality in the interests
of its circulation areas, which were referred to as 'Community'. At
the same time, the journalist set out to burnish his professional
image so that it imparted a sense of reliability, responsibility and a
spirit of truth-seeking. From these developments taken together,
it would seem that there was a remarkable coincidence of the public
or community interest with that of the newspaper business and
journalistic profession.

During the twentieth century, the advent of popular entertainment
and national mass media has led to a division of labour. Consequently
the local press has dropped many of its literary-type entertainment
features, the weeklies and bi-weeklies have become entirely local
in their coverage, and the evenings have a national/international
news coverage. Many local papers no longer run regular leaders
and their appearance and style has increasingly taken on that of the
impartial observer. The suspicion cannot have escaped the percep-
tive, however, that despite the vast preponderance in *Benn's Press
Directory*[3] of 'independent' local newspapers, these seem to be

consistently conservative in attitude as well as politically when they do editorialize. The argument in this book is that their seeming impartiality in news coverage inherently supports the status quo and is advantageous to locally powerful interests – of which more later.

Against this background, of the assertion of impartiality and the struggle for respectability, let us examine the performance of the press and consider some of the reasons that have been adduced for its weaknesses.

The Maud Report noted that 68 per cent of surveyed local voters mentioned the local newspaper as the most important source of news about local councils. Seventy-nine per cent said they read the local paper regularly. Only in London was the figure lower than 75 per cent. And 52 per cent of these voters wanted more information.[4] On the other hand, a study of interest groups in the Midlands by Newton and Morris of Birmingham University showed that the politically active put the local newspaper low on their list of priorities as a channel of political influence.[5] If the organizers of political pressure groups choose other means, direct negotiation with the local bureaucracy for instance, this question then arises: how effective is the press in making public important influences on local political decision-making, whose initiators do not regard the press as a significant element in the system of political power relations?

Evidence gleaned from analysis of newspaper content would suggest that it is not at all effective. As to the findings of content analysis inquiries, these do not seem to be of much consequence because, in as much as they do anything, they confirm common impressionistic judgements. This is hardly surprising, since they deal with a commodity which is easily and publicly available. In his study of the local press, A. J. Beith affirms that local authorities get about 16 per cent of coverage in the weeklies.[6] But the amount of coverage given to various local authorities does not correspond with their relative powers. County councils, which make fundamental decisions affecting rates, education, major roads, health services and planning get scant coverage compared with the affairs of the district or borough councils in the paper's circulation area.[7] This pathological parochialism has two aspects: not only does it set the value of the locality over and above that of larger, perhaps threatening, political units outside, but it also puts the integrity of local polity before sectional political interests. Typically, accounts of local affairs do not mention the political allegiance of councillors except at election times, and not always then. For instance, one local weekly carried an account on its front page of a row over the mayoralty, the crux of which was that an inter-party agreement on the annual alternation of the office had broken down because of the defeat of the Tory councillor at a local government election. But the story was written without reference to party allegiance, so that it was incomprehensible to anyone who did not already know who the dramatis personae were and to which parties they belonged.

Beith also remarks the lack of depth in reporting. Background information and fundamental causes are ignored. A story may give an account of a council's decision to initiate a given policy, but the source of the decision and the conflicts which surround it will not be revealed.

American studies indicate that the same tendency is manifested by the press in relation to local power interests. It seems that the local newspaperman is not the hard-hitting, fearless James Cagney who, we were led to believe, ran the American local press, setting up type with one hand, writing a devastating leader with the other, pausing only for a quick street fight with a small posse of local heavies. Instead, it transpires that the local weekly paper is unlikely to run stories which accentuate the notion of conflict within the community and that the local daily papers reflect the values of the dominant right-wing business community.[8] A study by an American academic, David L. Paletz, recounts the difference between the observations he and his assistants made at the city council meetings, and the accounts of these meetings which appeared subsequently in the local daily newspaper.[9] What was left out were those aspects of the council debates which would have made councillors look ridiculous: wrangles over procedural issues, public displays of ignorance, incompetent English corrected by reporters in writing up the stories. The overall impression given of the city council as a rational, ordered affair, was completely at variance with the reality. Of course the reporter's motives in such cases are entirely comprehensible. If he wrote up the story literally, verbatim, as it happened, no one would be able to follow it. If he explained what had happened and then gave accurate quotes from councillor's speeches, the resultant account would be so hilarious that the council would be outraged and probably cease any further co-operation. As it is, correcting councillor's grammar and verbal blunders becomes part of a reporter's second nature: he automatically translates the ubiquitous word 'irregardless' as 'regardless', eradicates double negatives generally, and substitutes 'imply' where necessary for 'infer'.

In one of the best-known studies of the American weekly press, *The Community Press in an Urban Setting*, Morris Janowitz finds its content to be bromide – or, as he puts it, 'community enhancing'.[10] The local weekly newspaper publisher in Chicago, according to this study, is very much an integral part of the local business community. He is likely to be an ex-advertising man, dress manufacturer, printer, or some other type of businessman, and to be from a family of high social status and economic class.

There is little point in labouring further the point that the content of the local press is harmless and non-controversial. But it is necessary to stress the sense in which this allegation is being made. It is not a question of the local press failing to editorialize for radical reform: no one in his right mind would expect the propagandists of big business to attack the basis of their own power and wealth. The basic criticism of this branch of the press is that the news it purveys as the allegedly impartial chronicle of events is an ideologically constructed version of reality, creating an image of local government which runs according to the rules and is manned only by benign, reasonable men. The much vaunted disinterested role in the functioning of democracy claimed by the journalist is a myth. Whatever his intention, the objective outcome of his activities is frequently propaganda for the status quo.

Let us look at some of the reasons adduced for the failure of the local press by a 'moderate' critic, A. J. Beith, who remains, nonetheless, within the traditional mainstream of liberal-democratic political philosophy, and the 'establishment' critic, Dilys Hill, whose book *Participating in Local Affairs*,[11] represents the establishment critical viewpoint of British local political processes.

Beith looks at what might be regarded as the stock criticisms of the local press, and comes up with the same sort of answers as did the 1949 and 1961 Royal Commissions.[12] These criticisms are that:

(a) the paramount commercial considerations prevent the press from fulfilling its responsibility, and
(b) the political commitment of individual newspapers causes them to fail to give 'a fair and representative account of politics at the local level'.

At its crudest, says Beith, the first argument is put in the form that newspapers are out to make money and are only interested in local government in as much as people are interested in it. Low polls at local elections indicate lack of interest and thus lack of prospective sales. Therefore, there is little coverage. He answers this criticism first with the naïve claim that editorial and commercial considerations are the realms of different departments and 'commercial calculation in newspapers may be made primarily by the non-journalistic executives, but it is the journalist who decides what to put in the paper'; except, that is, 'from time to time', when there are pressures to publish certain kinds of material, or to alter the balance or reader orientation of the paper. The result is a compromise between non-journalists and journalists 'who as a profession, have strong loyalties and traditions of responsibility'.

Secondly, he says, many local editors acknowledge an obligation to inform the electorate even though they regard active public interest as low. Third, he alleges that whatever commercial calculations they make about the saleability of local government news, they devote a great deal of space to it. Fourth, local government reporting does not need to be unprofitable, says Beith, and instances *The People* and corruption stories in support of this claim.

We shall be looking at all of these issues. For instance, as was indicated in the first chapter, the pervasiveness of commercial considerations is seen here as a prime quality of newspaper life. Journalists involved in the case referred in this book frequently expressed concern over such matters as explanations of editorial policy. Now of course editorial policy includes such matters of manning various types of story, and commercial considerations include freelance costs as well as advertising revenue. We shall also be concerned with the *type* of local government reporting rather than the simple *fact* of its being concerned with a given area of activity. Finally, we shall examine by example how valid is Beith's point about corruption stories being profitable. He equates profitability, seemingly, with high-revenue production: but the other element in profit calculation is cost. And when we examine the sort of cost elements involved in investigative reporting, Beith's assertion becomes highly questionable.

Beith also examines the influence of advertising as a more specific commercial pressure. He relies partly upon the Royal Commissions' findings that there was virtually no evidence of advertisers' pressure bringing about the suppression of reports, although he acknowledges that newspapers might be influenced by their own estimation of possible advertising revenue losses in selection of news material. Notions by editors that 'trouble is bad for trade' – or bad for tourism, for instance – might be put forward as causing biased news selection, but, says Beith, there is virtually no evidence of stories being deliberately buried because of considerations of this kind. Moreover, he adds, newspapers 'almost always' are ready to publish controversial material in the council chamber or public statements by, for instance, civic societies which are critical of trading interests. In considering this sort of belief about newspapers we shall be looking at a number of interesting examples of issues that were raised in council debates which were absent from the more important of the newspapers covering local affairs. Whether this had to do with the fact that the issues in question concerned the business interests of council members, one can only speculate.

As to the direct or indirect influence of advertisers, there are various ways in which such pressure can be successfully exerted on editors, journalists writing 'free puffs' to avoid clashes with big advertisers. But these are not the central, pervasive or characteristic influences of a journalist's life. To contend that there is virtually no evidence of suppression, however, tells us more about the methods of investigation employed by social science than about the influence of advertising. To expect practising editors or reporters to say honest-ly whether or not they are successfully pressured by advertisers is like asking a group of serving CID men whether they receive bribes from the underworld. The result is bound to be that few will admit to such a state of affairs. Whether this means the state of affairs does not exist or that the respondents or informants are covering up, is an open question.

Beith alleges that advertisers are likely to have only a slight influence on newspaper policy for two reasons. First, the nature of many of the advertisements (small ads and statutory notices) means that no one advertiser in the first case has any pull and in any case the advertisements are placed out of necessity, rather than charity. Second, he refers to the increasingly monopolistic position of the local weekly press which makes it difficult for an advertiser to pick and choose. The 1949 Royal Commission gives examples of advertisers' influence related to papers which were going to the wall in competitive situations. Such a process of reasoning appears to be based on the notion that the local paper deals with local adver-tisers exclusively. This is not so: the local weekly press deals with advertising agencies for much of its revenue. National advertisers make placings in local papers according to circulation figures for either individual papers or local newspaper chains. The local weekly paper is in no sense a monopolistic position vis-à-vis such advertisers. Further, these national sources, the statutory notices and local non-display advertisements, may constitute the background, regular sources of revenue on which a paper can rely, but profitabi-lity may well depend on the paper's ability to attract the local busi-ness advertiser: he may produce the marginal revenue to meet marginal costs. Thus he may be crucial to profitability.

So, according to Beith, direct or indirect commercial pressures do not account for the shortcomings of local journalism. Equally he finds that direct political commitment on the part of the news-paper itself is not an explanation for poor news coverage. More and more newspapers have abandoned direct political commitment over the years as a result of their passing out of family control, the influ-ence of the 'disinterested style' of radio and television, the effect of chain newspaper ownership, the decline of one-man ownership and the rise of the Labour Party in local government confusing old Liberal/Tory allegiances, Beith alleges.

The underlying assumption here is obviously an equation of political commitment with party support. It is possible to adopt a neutral stand vis-à-vis the two- or three-party system and still be committed to the dominant ideology of the political system. To be more explicit, there are a number of assumptions that support the political system which may well be enshrined more in the politically 'independent' newspaper than in those committed to one party: the notion that the civil service, local or national, is unbiased, professional and disinterested; that the courts are fair and just, and that the police are the instruments of society as a whole, dishonest policemen being a tiny minority – in short, that the governmental machine is not corrupt. The other part of this mythology may be summarized as follows: that there is a useful purpose in voting – it is a 'democratic duty', never mind whom you vote for, so long as you vote, that the politicians are all trying to do their best according to their beliefs, that moderation and the centre are desirable ends in themselves no matter what the few extremists and militants may suggest to the contrary; that within the usual traditions of the political gamut there is right on both sides – all those outside the gamut being misguided idealists or subversives. In short, that the electoral and legislative sectors of the political system are effective and are representative of society as a whole. Such a view, it seems, underlies the British national and local press, whether or not certain papers offer support to a particular party. And such a view seems to add up to a basic political commitment.

In her analysis of the relationship between the press and the local authority, Dilys Hill displays an extraordinary naïveté. The reason why the local authorities did not allow press coverage of their activities prior to the 'Thatcher Act' was not, she maintains, that they were 'deliberately trying to obstruct the press or evade the law'. And she attempts to qualify her contention in the following passage: 'First of all there was the problem of newspapers occasionally harassing officers. Second, local authorities complained that some papers tended to print only part of the information available, and this might distort the authority's side of an issue. Then there was the problem of papers which published confidential material. Finally there was a feeling of mistrust which was engendered when inexperienced reporters mis-reported information.'[13]

The councils are in a dilemma, she says. The activities which are likely to attract newspaper coverage are controversial matters of planning and compulsory purchase, but these are areas in which the local council is involved in financial and other negotiations with the affected parties 'and naturally feels that these discussions and preparations must take place in private. This is a basic conflict. The council believes that these decisions should not receive too much advance publicity, while the local paper feels that this is the only kind of local news of interest to the public. The council would prefer the paper to give publicity to the valuable – if routine – services while the paper wants to publicize the conflicts and controversies which emerge in local affairs'.[14]

At this point in Dr Hill's argument one is presented with the picture of a press seeking sensation, advance publicity, secret information. However, a little later, Dr Hill is arguing that what is wrong with the local press is that it does not 'probe' sufficiently. This, she says, is because of the number of young reporters who do not make personal contact with councillors to get background information. Instead, because their efforts are dispersed over a wide range of activities they are in a weak position to seek additional sources of news. They rely on council and official minutes when reporting on civic events. On the other hand, larger papers which can afford more staff employ more experienced staff on municipal affairs, and these reporters lobby councillors and municipal officials. In larger authorities councillors equally are more forthcoming with the press and the flow of information is continuous. To sum up this idyllic metropolitan scene, Dr Hill adds: 'The community benefits where a paper employs senior staff to gather local news. Councillors appreciate that they are dealing with *responsible* reporters who can distinguish between *official* facts and personal opinions, and who will respect the *confidentiality of background information*'.[15]

It is hard to decide which kind of bad newspaper Dr Hill has in mind as characteristic of the British local press – the officer-harassing, sensation-mongering rag or the stodgy parish-pump weekly full of misreported accounts of council meetings written by juniors. It is apparent, on the other hand, that what she regards as a happy state of affairs is one in which reporters who are dubbed 'responsible' by authority publish a special variety of 'fact' that has 'official' approval and at the same time respect the 'confidentiality of background information'. One wonders how scandals such as the Poulson affair or the Sheffield Police case ever came to light – certainly it could not have been through the efforts of Dr Hill's confidential watchdogs.

If we look to Beith's analysis of the shortcomings of press coverage of local political affairs we find a similar confusion and ~~pussyfooting~~ around the issues. Having referred earlier to the fact that news reporters often know the background to municipal stories but do not include it in their reports, he suggests that one of the reasons for the failure of the local press is that young reporters are of poor quality and do not have the opportunity to gain a good background knowledge of town-hall affairs. The reasons for this sorry state are, he says, as follows. First, few local weekly papers can afford to pay the salaries which their best reporters get by moving on to evenings or nationals. Second, rates of pay in journalism outside Fleet Street are low and do not compete with industry or the professions. Only in the Thomson Organization did Beith meet graduates (this is a strange argument: Thomson wages are no better than other papers of similar size). Third, understaffing causes reliance on lineage and freelance agencies, with consequent lack of continuity. Fourth, few local papers can afford a special correspondent on local affairs. The latter two arguments are most peculiar. More often than not it is the local weekly reporter who works as a freelance, selling lineage about the local area to the nationals. Moreover, all local weekly newspapermen are special correspondents on local affairs, for they spend every day of their working lives in the area.

Beith also refers to the effects of newspaper practice and identifies the limitations of traditional local journalism; the conservatism of the trade; and the reluctance to accept graduates as factors accounting for the parlous state of the trade. He also refers to the 'office diary' which, he alleges, prevents reporters from getting specialist training by dispersing their activities randomly over diary engagements. The effects of this lack of specialization are increased by the lack of opportunity to use knowledge if it were acquired, coupled with a lack of general knowledge and understanding of local government by reporters. This is explained by the older journalists' traditional formalistic training of young reporters which concentrates on journalistic structures rather than accounts of what actually happens. Says Beith: 'The most effective limitations of the reporting of local government are not external, nor are they such often criticized features of newspaper control as political commitment or unwillingness to deal with subjects with no obvious commercial appeal. They are aspects of the very traditional practice of journalism as it is carried on in most newspaper offices.'

The views of Beith and Hill, it is argued here, are naïve and based upon a rarified unwillingness to do anything so ungentlemanly as to question the accounts actors give of themselves. In the event, it is easier to blame the incompetence of those young, ignorant, nongraduate junior reporters and their unsatisfactory training schemes. This is simply not good enough. Some of their arguments are based on simple ignorance. For instance, on all the weekly papers whose procedures the author has observed, the 'diary' does not have the effect alleged by Beith. Reporters do tend to specialize in their own area and have their own councils to cover. More importantly, if young journalists are trained to work in a particular way in the context of an economically motivated organization, one must ask why. Whom does it benefit to have a neutered press? Who are the people who own the press? How are the relationships between editorial staff and administrators in newspaper firms actually negotiated? We shall also examine the sort of information that councils make available before decisions are made. Consideration of the nature of some 'official facts' gives rise to the hypothesis that bureaucratic versions of events are more to do with the organizational survival of bureaucrats than with the provision of information, however defined for the public. Further, the secretive tendencies of local government seem to result at times in the obfuscation of such matters as councillors' financial interests, through the operation of the very rules which are supposed to preserve the merits of the system.

PART TWO

The reporter 'on the beat'

3
Pluralism and protest groups

Political Science provides us with a model of liberal democratic politics which is an amalgam of prescription and myth, but which carries great force and, occasionally, impinges on to reality. In the recent debate about the free press and the danger of the closed shop, for instance, the ideal state of the freedom of the press and the present reality of oligopolistic competition between privately owned giants were noiselessly elided so that myth and reality were impossible to distinguish. In modern democratic theory, according to such denizens as Robert Dahl,[1] Joseph Schumpeter,[2] Polsby[3] and Samuel Finer,[4] there is competition between élites in a market type situation in which the voter like the customer is king. Periodically the voter puts the stamp of approval or disapproval on the élite in power. Between these electoral tournaments the press is the means by which the voter is informed of the processes of government and by which he is exposed to the numerous ideas about politics from which he is to choose. The free, private enterprise press provides a 'free market in ideas'. Freedom of thought and the private ownership of property, in the shape of newspaper publishing combines, are thus compounded as the inseparable ingredients of a free, democratic society. But another process also takes place between elections. Pressure groups, the bodily incarnation of the spirit of pluralism, intervene between the government and the governed, providing the government with vital information about the needs and aspirations of the populace to which it can then respond, and the populace in turn with the chance to take part in the political process and to influence government. The government and the civil service in this best of all possible worlds are referees, dispassionate arbitrators between competing interests, none of whose interests they represent.[5]

This profoundly ideological view of the political process is often put forward as pristine empiricism. Robert Dahl in *Who Governs?*, for instance, presents an analysis of the alleged processes of government in an American city which is based almost entirely on the accounts of participants, whose meanings are not questioned. The nature of reality is apparently unproblematic. Samuel Finer in *Anonymous Empire* seems to find the essential goodness of the British political system empirically demonstrable. Interest groups with their sectional interests are confronted by government institutions: 'They counter the centrifugal demands of the sectional groups. They domesticate them. They amalgamate with them to produce government which is, all in all, still honest, humane and just.' The civil service, in contrast to the self-interested pressure group, is seen as 'disinterested, aloof, critical and dispassionate'. Even the political parties are seen as 'goodies'. 'Party politics is not a naked coalition of sectional interests. The parties have to *democratize* the claims of such interests.' For Finer, the argument that poor pressure groups cannot mobilize resources as well as those possessing wealth 'does not impress', and the only pressure-group power which does concern him is that of the trade union.[6]

Now this is a view of the liberal-democratic political system which, although killed on a number of occasions, will not lie down. Like Lazarus it has a lot of loving relatives and friends who invoke divine influence to revive it. Even now in its newly sanctified form of anti-extremism and 'moderation' it wanders about the land stubbing its toes on a Poulson here a T. Dan Smith there, a slagheap. It is interesting that certain labels such as 'extremist' and 'moderate' are accepted as appropriate factual categories for social scientists, A. J. M. Sykes and I. Illersic seeing this as an acceptable and apparently desirable way of studying the complexities of British trade unionism.[7] From a conventional standpoint in the 1960s it would have been held absurd to claim that British civil servants might well have their hands in the till, or that an American president might use burglars to plant evidence on his opponents or use his position to fiddle his tax, or that the CIA would deliberately 'destabilize' a political system which had freely elected a left-wing government, or that Hong Kong police inspectors might use their position to become dollar millionaires. Such views would have been considered 'extremist'.

Let us now examine two cases of attempts by pressure groups to convince the local press and local government of the truth of such an 'extremist' position: a challenge to the good faith of local politicians. In doing so we shall examine the processes by which a given view of political life and given political activities are labelled deviant, and excluded from the consensus-oriented arena of respectable pressure groups. As a consequence we shall see that the pluralist view of politics is inadequate to explain these processes: not because pluralism is ethically unsatisfactory – that is of no interest here – but analytically unviable. This is because it accepts the type-categories of the proponents of a particular ideology as its own terms of analysis, and denies the existence of non-conforming reality except as the receptacle of abuse. Indeed a consensus-pluralist view of politics is one of the resources of the agencies of government in dealing with protest groups and one of the resources of the respectable protest group in gaining recognition by the other participants in the local game of established politics.

The first case study concerns the events surrounding a successful planning application by a councillor; the second, a conflict between a councillor's business interests and his role as a local politician and worthy. In neither case did the attempts of local protesters result in the local press taking up the campaign, by investigating the facts.

The Marlborough Drive conspiracy theorists

By profession councillor Tommy Simon is a builder. In the normal course of events he buys and sells land in Smallborough where his brother, who works in the family business, is also on the council. They have generally both been members of the council, but when Tommy Simon was voted off for two years his brother Jack Simon remained on the council, representing a different ward. During this sojourn Tommy Simon devoted his energies to his own business and to charitable good works which sometimes seemed to coincide with it.

In 1971 Smallborough Urban District Council had a town centre redevelopment scheme which was to be financed by the property developers Euroshops Trust. On the perimeter of this exciting new scheme the planners envisaged a new public park which Small-borough, filled with the débris of the Industrial Revolution, plainly lacked. A local grocer called Henry Thorn, seeing that the end of the small business concern in the town was imminent, decided to sell his main street shop and the derelict 2-acre site behind his house in Marlborough Drive and retire on the proceeds. In order to do this with the greatest profit he applied to the council for permission to develop the vacant site with new houses. The council turned down his application on the grounds that the site was required for part of their scheduled 6-acre park, which was to be included in the re-planned town centre. Not only would this land provide some of the public open space which the town lacked, but would also serve as playing fields for nearby schools. Jack Braine, a neighbour of Thorn, decided he would like to buy the house and the land in the hope of redeveloping it, but it then came to light through inquiries made by his solicitor that the land was blighted by the council's plans for the area. Thorn now wrote to the council asking it to remove his land from the development scheme or buy it and the house from him. At this point Simon intervened and offered Thorn more than Braine, on the chance that the council would decide against using the land. Thorn accepted and Simon's building firm became the owner of the land.

In addition to his business and political work, Simon contributed further to the public benefaction of Smallborough as a trustee of the

Ramsbottom Trust, a local charity set up by the originator of Smallborough's growth, Sir Seth Ramsbottom, a Methodist and mill-owner. This trust was originally for the relief of the temperate poor who had been laid destitute usually by Sir Seth's business activities. One of the schemes in hand was to move the inmates of Ramsbottom House which was due for demolition to modern buildings. All of the inmates were old-age pensioners, most of them temperate old ladies.

The Ramsbottom Trust wrote to the council offering to buy the vacant 2-acre site in Marlborough Drive for the purpose of rehousing the inmates of the poorhouse in nineteen modern bungalows and building a warden's lodge. This was the only vacant site near the centre of Smallborough which could satisfactorily replace the present accommodation. The temperate ladies who would live there would serve to represent some of those for whom the public open space had been intended, and the layout of grounds, which were to be maintained professionally, would blend in with the park. The redevelopment sub-committee advised the council to accept the request on the advice of the town surveyor.

The owners of the land, Tommy Simon Builders Ltd, now made a planning application for the redevelopment of the site with twenty single-bedroom bungalows, and, since the redevelopment sub-committee had withdrawn its interest, the planning committee approved the application subject to conditions to protect the amenities and character of the area. The Ramsbottom Trust then bought the land.

During the negotiations with the redevelopment sub-committee, the Ramsbottom Trust had merely said that it wished to purchase the land, depending on the removal of the planning restriction. No one had mentioned that the owner of the land, at the time at which the issue was raised, was none other than the former council member Tommy Simon. Jack Simon, his brother, who was a member of the redevelopment sub-committee and a co-director of Simon's building firm, made no mention of the firm's interest in the land. Having bought the land without planning permission Simon was able to sell it as land which was ripe for development and therefore worth several times the amount he had paid for it. Yet all that appeared in the published epitome of the minutes of Smallborough Council was the original decision to lift the blight on the land, without the names of the owners, and three months later a planning permission to T. Simon for development of the land at the rear of The Gables, Marlborough Drive, the local press made no connection between the two and probably nothing further would have been said about the matter had it not been for the sense of injury felt by Jack Braine.

Jack Braine was a member of the local church, of the Smallborough Protection Society, which had been set up to protect the town against the schemes of Euroshops, and of the local Liberal Party. However, if Braine was one of the rank and file, his friend and neighbour, the doughty Flora Duddon, was a general. Her husband Bill was a local chartered surveyor and also a member of the Ramsbottom Trust, in which capacity he discovered that Simon was the owner of the land on which the bungalows were to be built. Mrs Duddon told Jack Braine, who then realized that the man who had gazzumped him was a well-known local worthy and landlord who had subsequently sold the land at a profit because of the change in planning permission. Mrs Duddon told several of her neighbours, including another member of the Smallborough Liberal Association, Mrs Allen. Mrs Allen was quick to divine a conspiracy and put the different pieces of the puzzle together. Tommy Simon had bought the land along with Thorn's house with the benefit of inside information from his brother for £10,000 and had sold it for £30,000. The figure of £10,000 came from Thorn's wife who had a bad conscience about Braine being gazzumped in the first place. She was an old friend of Mrs Braine, Mrs Allen and Mrs Duddon and a key link in the intense gossip-network centred at the junction of Marlborough Drive and the neighbouring George Street. The figure of £30,000 came up as the story circulated around the network. Mrs Thompson's husband, who worked in the county council estates and valuation office, had said that the land must have been worth at least £30,000 with planning permission.

It is important to note at this point the process by which a hypothesis about the actual profit made by Simon came to be supported and accepted as valid fact. If it had been possible to obtain £30,000 for property, it was argued, Simon would certainly have got it. In the contacts made with the redevelopment sub-committee no mention had been made of Simon's ownership of the land. The Ramsbottom Trust secretary must have known, so either the town clerk had been in on the deal or had been duped. If, it was reasoned, Simon had not been up to something, if he had bought the land in order to hold it by prior arrangement for the Ramsbottom Trust for instance, there would have been no need for him to keep quiet about his interest in the land. The fact that he had not mentioned his ownership of the land was taken as proof of his bad intentions, while the interpretation of his silence as deliberate was inferred from the assumption that he was a sharp businessman, i.e., that he had bad intentions.

In other words the process by which a hypothesis came to be validated was circular and exclusive of alternatives. Questions were begged by positing the implicit ridiculous alternative. It seemed to an observer that this circulatory relationship between ideology and reality drew its strength from the social relationships which existed between the Braines, the Thorns, the Allens, the Duddons and the Thompsons. Not only did they live close together, which meant that the wives met frequently and formulated a common perception of various events. This geographical proximity was overlaid by common activities – membership of the Liberal Association and of the church, participation in the church play-ground organization – and Mr Braine and Mr Allen were both engineers at a nearby commercial vehicle company. Not all the members of the gossip-network were bound by such multiple ties, but no two participants were connected by less than two areas of activity.

In this context a version of reality and its ethical significance is established as a unity. The protagonists do not say 'Simon paid £2,000 more than Jack Braine offered, got the land, persuaded the council to change the planning permission and then sold it to the Ramsbottom Trust, of which he is a member', and then move to interpret the significance of these statements in the light of other evidence. The fact that a certain sequence of events occurred is regarded of itself as irrefutable evidence of malice aforethought. This process of empirical verification combined with ethical judgement could even generate the sale price of £30,000 for the land. There appeared to be a powerful connection between this 'conspiracy theory' ideology and the interaction among its proponents, which as we shall see was further reinforced by their exclusion from taking other political action. Such processes in sociological literature have been associated with isolated members of the working class, such as coalminers who are held to be peculiarly prone to striking, and with certain political attitudes which are at variance with those of the dominant consensus. However, the evidence in this case suggests that the social processes associated with conflict-oriented politics are not determined by class – the Marlborough Drive group was comprised of professional workers and suburban dwellers – nor by physical isolation from the pressures of the rest of society, as Kerr and Siegal seem to suggest.[8] They lived and interacted among people of various views which were generally different from their own. Furthermore, they were a type of 'radical', in that they effectively rejected a consensus view of politics in a particular case, which some of them generalized to the overall political system. But their radicalism was not that of the soul-searching 'wet Liberal', heavily tainted with goodness, which emerged from Frank Parkin's *Middle Class Radicalism*.[9] There was a strong sense of personal grievance and attack usually associated with right- and left-wing 'extremism'.

The Marlborough Drive group, especially Mrs Duddon and Mr Braine, wanted to expose what they regarded as a piece of chicanery and they attempted to articulate their protest through three established channels: political parties and councillors; local pressure groups; the press and broadcasting. Each of these established channels failed to produce the results they desired, until an apparently chance coincidence of circumstances brought about coverage by a local television news programme. It became evident that the basis on which the channels of established protest and publicity were denied to the protesters was not that their allegations were weighed by specialists in the media, or by politically powerful individuals, and found wanting as an item of news or subject of moral concern. Nor could the personal prejudices of the individual protagonists be summoned as an explanation, a theory called into play by Manning White and the other 'gatekeeper' theorists[10] in their newspaper studies. What appeared to be the case was that the 'consensus', 'moderate' establishment ideology of the individuals in gatekeeper positions (those who were able to include or exclude the issue as a viable news story or as legitimate grievance politically) involved the same circulatory process of validation as that of the conspiracy theorists of Marlborough Drive. The difference was that while physical proximity and dense social interaction ruled out any official opposition to the conspiracy theorists' perception of a particular set of events, in the consensus situation competitive perceptions of particular events were allowed and arbitrated according to the normal rules of negotiation. But even in the latter case perceptions challenging the validity of the system (i.e. the rules) or the good faith of participants were excluded. Now obviously this at times involved a difficulty, because occasionally an individual's motives are impugned, but the only allowance for public acknowledgement of this is when it is done by established agencies – the courts and the police. In other words, the impugning of the individual's motives no longer calls in question the integrity of the system. Indeed it might even be argued that it strengthens the system by reassuring the beliefs of the majority and categorizing the rotten apple in the barrel as an isolated deviant.[11]

It would of course be wrong to regard ideology as a purely psychological or individual characteristic. Rather, it can be seen as arising from the actions of individuals in given social and organizational contexts and as providing them with the means to perceive and construct reality in a way which legitimates their own positions vis-à-vis the distribution of power, wealth, prestige and other values. In order to investigate the way in which perceptions and constructions arise out of social processes, let us examine the consensus, moderate establishment ideology processes as they responded to the agitation of the Marlborough Drive conspiracy theorists.

Political parties and councillors

A number of Labour councillors were approached as the story of the Simon land deal spread along the network of gossip around the Smallborough town centre. Mr Allen contacted Councillor Brown, a work colleague of his, and he inquired about the matter through the town hall. Having investigated the affair, the councillor wrote to Mr Allen saying that there did appear to have been a mistake made at the town hall, although he did not specify what it was, but that nothing illegal had been done. Councillor Brown appeared to be unable or unwilling to take any further steps, and at this point he left the story. Except, that is, for the fact that Mr Braine photocopied the letter.

Mrs Duddon told Kate Mather, a young woman social worker and Smallborough Protection Society activist who lived in Wolfe Road, off Marlborough Drive that Simon the builder and ex-Independent member of Smallborough Council had bought a piece of land for £10,000 arranged for a planning restriction to be removed and then sold it to a charitable trust of which he was a member for three times the amount of purchase.

Kate and her husband Bill were both active members of the local Labour Party and were on close terms with a number of the few Labour councillors on the town and county councils. They discussed that matter and decided that if it were true it was a monumental fiddle and needed exposing. They asked Ron Dunning, the chairman of the planning committee, to look into it for them. He inquired at the town clerk's department and at the planning office and was told 'the facts' as they had been depicted in the council minutes. However, he produced for the Mathers a photocopy of a map, the planning application, the clerk's report to the redevelopment sub-committee, the planning officer's report, and a copy of a letter from the solicitor of the Ramsbottom Trust, who was also Simon's solicitor and sometime business partner, requesting the removal of the planning permission and disserting on the worthy and humane purposes to which the land was to be put.

Mr Mather had additional copies made of these documents, and yet further blotchy photostats were fed into the network. Mr Braine, the Duddons and Mrs Allen had copies, and they were circulated among everyone in the small circle. However, Councillor Dunning's message for the Mathers was simple: nothing can be done; no illegality has been perpetrated, although Mr Simon may have been guilty of sharp practice. The Mathers who were Roman Catholics approached a co-religionist, Councillor Tommy Fitzgibbon, without much hope that he could achieve anything. Mrs Mather felt that he never understood the complexities of the case, and after a fortnight he reported back that there was no truth in the rumours about Tommy Simon, who by this time had been re-elected to the council.

Finally, the chairman of the Smallborough Protection Society approached Councillor Bob Major who, after investigating the affair through the bureaucracy, reported that although Simon had evidently been sailing close to the wind, he was far too wily to be caught doing anything illegal. The chairman of the protection society accepted this, but Mrs Allen hastened to point out to the Marlborough Drive group that Councillor Major had left his wife to live round the corner with a lady magistrate. How could a man in such a personal tangle impugn another councillor's morality? His own position was such that he was very vulnerable to a whispering campaign. Fear of being 'nobbled' in the next year's council elections was assigned the cause of his silence.

None of these deadlocks could persuade the Marlborough Drive group that there was no basis for their case. The Mathers, who were accepted as trustworthy allies, wrote off Fitzgibbon as a simpleton; Major was a paper tiger because of his moral vulnerability; and the others were 'no use' or 'all backing one another'. In other words the councillors' rejection of the group's view of the events simply added grist to the mill. It showed that not only were some politicians dishonest but that they were able to rely on the fear, stupidity and compliance of others in order to practise their deceits.

The sentence in Councillor Brown's letter referring to a mistake at the town hall was seized on as an admission that something was wrong. The logic behind this assumption was that if something had gone wrong at the town hall it must obviously have involved the officials there. Strange it was that this mistake (as yet unspecified) should have benefited Tommy Simon to the tune of £20,000. The explanation: someone in a sufficiently influential position to affect the writing of a town clerk's report was a Mr Fixit for Tommy Simon. Several heads were tried for size to see if the cap fitted. None was rejected on the grounds of improbability, but there was no clue to differentiate one almost certainly guilty party from another. It was not simply that they received only information supporting their own hypothesis as was the case in Festinger's experiments on perception, but also that pieces of information, in themselves neutral, were processed into manifestoes of ideological potency. Where individuals such as Festinger's subjects[12] had to select appropriate messages on the basis of their own internal processes, the Marlborough Drive group could rely on the mutual support of like-minded neighbours nursing a common sense of grievance. Any threat to the security of their perception or a hint of 'cognitive dissonance' was swept aside by a communal certainty and an infallible process of validation.

Other direct approaches to the political party system were made through the Smallborough Liberal Association. Mr Braine raised the issue at his ward meeting. Mr Allen contacted Ralph White, a local Liberal candidate who had been a member of the council for a term during the Orpington revival period. White said the matter needed looking into, especially in view of the large number of people among the ranks of Tory and Independent members of the council who were estate agents and builders, and did nothing. Nothing at all came from the approaches of the protesters to the established political party channels. What was significant about the actions of the councillors involved was that when faced with a challenge to the probity of a local politician and possibly to local municipal officials, they went to the council bureaucracy to check the truth of the allegations. There was an implicit belief in the probity of the system which begged the question which they supposedly wanted to answer: had the local government machine been subverted for profit by Tommy Simon, his brother or local officials?

Councillor Dunning said afterwards that although Simon could not be trusted, he was too clever a man to do anything illegal. Simon was a good councillor and a clever committee man. The officials at the town hall had said that nothing illegal had taken place and Dunning accepted this. The question of whether something could have been done which was legal in a strict sense of the word but could have meant taking advantage of political influence, and therefore worthy of exposure, was not considered. Legality pure and simple was selected as the framework of relevance.

Local pressure groups

The Smallborough Protection Society was a general amenity group which was particularly concerned at this time with opposition to the Euroshops scheme. Mrs Allen raised the issue at one of the society's general meetings. Her chief limitation was that her style of oratory was so cryptic that what she meant was not always apparent to those who were unfamiliar with the facts of the matter. There were, she said, 'certain land deals' being undertaken by 'certain members of the council' and large profits were being made out of these deals which arose directly as a result of the Euroshops redevelopment scheme, which the council were backing. This speech formed part of a debate on what to do about the town centre scheme, and although it contained no proposals for action, it was clapped enthusiastically by the Marlborough Drive conspiracy theorists, others who knew vaguely about the case, and a group of old ladies living in some doomed cottages who clapped whenever anyone accused a councillor of taking a 'back hander'.

Mr Braine became a member of the management committee of the society, and raised the matter under 'any other business'. He was very concerned to prove that something underhand had been done: either that Simon had used inside information about the reduction in the demand for public open space by the council to his own advantage, or that pressure had been brought to bear to get the council to change its planning decision and thus profit Simon. Mr Braine rehearsed all the details of the case, including the minutiae of the gazzumping, but, not being an experienced speaker, frequently lost his way. His immediate effect on the committee was to bring an embarrassing silence, but Mrs Duddon, who was also a member, charged to Mr Braine's rescue. Was the society just there for opposition to council schemes or was it there to protect Smallborough, she asked. Private schemes, sales of large pieces of land near the town centre, were just as likely to change the place as council schemes, only there was even less control by the public over the course of development. The society should at least look into it. The chairman, Jed Roper, a local headmaster, got in touch with Bob Major, with the results described above.

Again, when interviewed, Roper repeated that there was nothing illegal in what Simon had done, although he was basing this judgement entirely on Major's inquiries and interpretation of events. When it was suggested that it was possible for private developers to redevelop the whole town without actually doing anything illegal, he said he did not see that there was anything that the protection society could do about it. The society developed a negotiating relationship with the town-hall bureaucracy, and Roper saw the role of the pressure group as that of a trade union in an orderly 'collective bargaining' situation. To 'legality' as a circumscription for relevance can be added the boundaries of the political universe laid down by the bureaucratic structures of various government agencies. In relation to legality as a criterion, the interesting characteristic was that its definition depended either on non-legal authorities, local councillors, or upon the advice of professionals who, it could reasonably be assumed, might possibly have an interest in the case: the local bureaucracy.

The press and broadcasting

When these approaches appeared to be having no effect Mrs Duddon decided that the time had come to approach the press and the other media with a story which, she believed, as contacts often do when they are fired by their own cause, the press would jump at. However, they did not do so and the reasons for this are worth examining.

Smallborough did not have its own newspaper. Several nearby

weeklies had tried to move in with special Smallborough editions or even Smallborough pages, but had failed. The town's own weekly newspaper, the *Smallborough City Times*, had died during the 1950s. One of the causes of its demise, apart from the small population of the town and the fact that people living in peripheral areas tended to be drawn to other neighbouring centres, was that there was a regional evening paper covering a number of towns and having the quality of several small papers rolled into one. This newspaper, the *Midnorth Evening Gazette*, gave substantial space to small classified advertisements and the businessmen of Smallborough generally advertised in it. It had a little office in Smallborough used by the local reporter who covered the whole town, but mainly the council and the magistrates' court. The office was permanently attended by a receptionist who took in advertisements and passed on information to the reporter, Dave Jary, when he called there to write up or phone through his stories to the head office at Longtown.

Mrs Duddon arranged to see Jary and took the papers which showed the refusal of planning permission to Thorn, and the granting of the permission to Simon, along with the appeal to the redevelopment sub-committee on behalf of the Ramsbottom Trust. Jary said he would look into it and Mrs Duddon never heard any more from him. It is unclear why he abandoned his inquiries, but it is not surprising in view of his method of working and the amount he was required to cover. His office was next door to the town hall and a short walk from the magistrates' court. These were his two main sources of news. In covering the council affairs he would scan the minutes and take up any likely item with one of the council officials, most of whom he had known for many years. Many of them had much shorter working lives in association with Smallborough Council. Jary was something of a regular in the town hall. If he saw any building-work demolition or other signs of activity in the town which had not appeared in the minutes he would check it out with the appropriate official. Such a move had once led to a successful campaign to save a local hall from being demolished. He also had a number of councillors and other local politicians as 'contacts' who could be relied to tip him off about forthcoming council decisions, internal party splits and a variety of other items which were regarded as 'good' stories. The editor of the *Midnorth Evening Gazette* said that Dave Jary knew more about what was going on in Smallborough than most of the council: he was a first-class local reporter.

Jary did not mix much with council officials or politicians outside his working life. But he regarded his relationships with them as friendly, and plainly the successful execution of his job required the co-operation of a number of councillors and local officials. It did not involve investigation of council affairs. 'Checking' simply meant finding out what was happening according to one of the people engaged in executing or laying down council policy. This might include conflict where it was of the inter-party or intra-party type prescribed by consensus politics. And, of course, the daily coverage of the court and the regular coverage of council affairs, along with any stories about hundredth birthdays or golden weddings which were brought in and could not be palmed off on to a junior at Longtown head office, more or less precluded spending time on investigative reporting. Town hall officials, Jary found, were generally co-operative, some of them very clever, and honest if at times dictatorial. Councillors were also generally honest, some were awkward, some generally capable, but rarely as intelligent as the officials. Many were in it for political glory, which made his job easier because they loved publicity, but in his experience they were not in it for personal economic gain. He was not predisposed to believe tales of town-hall corruption. But then, of course, he had never been looking for it.

Mrs Allen now sought to get the drama played on a national stage. She thought the campaigning clarion of the nation's liberal conscience would take up her cause. Accordingly she telephoned an acquaintance who worked as a writer on *The Guardian* and told him her story. She said he told her that *The Guardian* did not cover local stories but that she should write to the letters-to-the-editor column as the appropriate channel for getting redress of these wrongs. She wrote, but nothing happened. This was not difficult to understand. She launched into her letter by saying that 'concern was being felt among the residents of Smallborough' as if all the world would know where the town was. And then, quite apart from its parochialism, the letter was cryptic to the point of conveying nothing at all specific. It related a 'London based property company', the innocent Euroshops, to Simon's land deal, which was pluralized along with Simon to become 'speculative property deals by local councillors'. These property deals were in turn linked with council health department surveys of local housing in preparation of clearance areas. The underlying plot, which was supposed to explain a whole series of apparently disparate events, thus involved the council as a body, but especially some money-making members and the inspectors of the public health department, in a conspiracy to redevelop the centre of Smallborough for their own personal profit.

Now editors generally set considerable store by letters from readers as sources of news, but the kind of information they require is that which fits into the mini-max model of the good news story. It should provide the basis for a story with good readership pull, or maximum returns, which demands the minimum labour time and expenses – and naturally excludes the risk of libel cases or the closing of useful future sources of news, from councillors or officials. Mrs Allen's letter would have been inappropriate for the letter column or as a news source for a national newspaper since it was not only parochial but cryptic. But even if it had been clear and related to some nationally relevant issue, it would still have failed the mini-max test. Assuming it had had an acceptable readership pull and that the costs in terms of time and journalists' expenses were satisfactory, the libel costs could have been prohibitive. These incidents, it should be noted, took place before the Poulson bankruptcy hearings and the *Washington Post* Watergate campaign had made 'investigative journalism' fashionable in Britain.

In dealing with the local newspaper Mrs Duddon had faced the additional difficulty that her story was a one-off job which constituted a potential threat to the future regular supply of news. Whereas Mrs Allen decided that *The Guardian* did not after all care about little people and gave up her attempts to get press coverage, Mrs Duddon persisted by making approaches to other media. Dave Jary, she decided, was 'in with them', despaired of the press and moved on to a local television programme, *Civil Rights*, which was specifically a channel of protest for local people with a gripe against the council, businesses and government. She contacted the programme's anchor man Len Baric, who asked her for more information: What was the date of the first sale? Who exactly was the owner of the land at the time of the planning permission being granted? Had Simon's brother voted on the planning decision? Mrs Duddon suggested that the television company send a representative to see Mr Braine. In the meantime she met Mrs Thorn, who told her that her husband regretted having sold the land to Simon and would do what he could to help. Mrs Duddon said that information as to who exactly had bought the land and when would be very much appreciated.

The television reporter, Peter Martin, was a young man hoping to make his way in the company and had been taken on on a temporary trial basis. He interviewed Mr Braine and took all the documents which he had relating to the proposed sale of the land to him by Thorn. Martin then called on Mrs Duddon, who told him in much more concise terms what had transpired and why she thought that Simon was a scoundrel. She also told Martin that Mrs Thorn and probably her husband would speak to him. Mr Thorn told Martin that Braine was a fool and could have had the land if he had not dithered, but said that Simon was a scoundrel, and confirmed the facts of the sale to him.

Martin, who had recorded the interviews, told the programme controller for local programmes that he thought the subject would be good for news feature coverage rather than the more advice-oriented *Civil Rights* programme. The paper he had been given showed that the owner of the land was not Thomas Simon, the individual, but Thomas Simon Ltd the builder. It also showed that the land in question was not one plot but several. The programme editor, John Hutchinson, passed on the papers, of which two more sets of photocopies were now made, to the company solicitors. They said that there was a *prima facie* case for further inquiries to ascertain who owned Thomas Simon Builders Ltd, and how much the Ramsbottom Trust had paid Simon for the land. In relation to the land's status they said that in view of the description of the land in the land registry draft documents provided by Mr Thorn, it was not clear as to which site the planning permission referred. It mentioned 'Land fronting on to Marlborough Drive adjacent to number 29', but only one of the plots actually fronted the drive.

The Ramsbottom Trust was registered with the Registry of Friendly Societies, but a search there by another reporter, Trevor McKenzie, showed that the annual returns were not yet available and the Trust's previous annual returns had contained no details of land transactions: it was not possible to get the figure without a direct approach to Simon. McKenzie at this point was offered a job in London and left. He had made a written request to Company House for information about the ownership and officers of Thomas Simon Ltd, Builders. This showed that of the company's available share issue of 1,000, 103 had actually been taken up. Thomas Simon owned a hundred, his wife one, and his brother and sister-in-law one each. The brother was also a director and had drawn £500 in fees at the last count for his services. This meant that when the planning restriction on the land had come up for review and when the planning application had been considered he should have declared an interest, provided of course that he had been present at the council when the committee reports were voted on or in committee when the votes were taken. Failure to declare such an interest is normally a criminal offence. A second firm of solicitors who provided the advice in the *Civil Rights* programme were consulted. They advised checking the brother's attendance record to see if he had been at the meetings.

At this point Martin's trial period came to an end and Hutchinson decided not to renew his contract. When the author interviewed Hutchinson shortly afterwards he said that the Simon story was holding fire until they knew what had been paid for the land by the Ramsbottom Trust. What he did not say was that Martin had been dismissed. Nor did he make any indication that the file, the tape recordings and some short pieces of film done on the story had all disappeared. A few weeks later Hutchinson himself left for a better job and the film remained unmade. After another year of inactivity, having decided that the film was now unlikely to be made, the author

called on Councillor Oldfield, the new chairman of the redevelopment sub-committee who, it turned out, was no friend of Simon.

On being asked if it was true that Simon and his brother were
owners of the land in question, if the brother had voted on an issue
in which he had a business interest, and how much the land had been
sold for, Councillor Oldfield reacted strongly. Moreover, he raised
the issue at the submission of his next sub-committee report and
requested an inquiry by the town clerk's department into the circumstances of the change of planning permission and the change in
the requirement for public open space in the town centre redevelopment. The day after the council meeting he telephoned to say that
Simon had threatened libel actions against people who were 'spread-
ing rumours' about him in relation to other affairs associated with
his activities as a landlord. Oldfield was worried and wanted some
evidence to be produced. Eventually the papers were traced and
Councillor Oldfield was handed proof that at the time the decision
was taken by the council to lift the planning blight Thomas Simon
Builders Ltd, was the owner of the land.

The town clerk's report when it appeared was something of a
mouse: it did not go into the issue of the declaration of personal
interest by Simon's brother who, it transpired, had not been at
either meeting when the relevant votes were taken. Simon refused to
say how much had been paid for the land, and Councillor Oldfield
said that in future all reports on such matters should contain the
names of the owners and have specific information as to the exact
titles of such land. In any event, the report was kept confidential.
When it was presented to the public council meeting one of the
members of the council who was not involved declared that the
report was 'dynamite' and that if the press got hold of it it would
provide the basis of a 'character assassination'. The press should
not be allowed to get hold of a copy, he maintained. At the same
time a new reporter at the television company, Bob Ferguson, was
following up the Simon story once again and obtained photocopies
of my documents from me before furthering his enquiries.

The reporters from the *Midnorth Evening Gazette* and from the
area freelance agency, Longtown News Services, sat impassive at the
press bench. Ferguson, however, already had a copy of the town
clerk's report, which he had obtained from a town-hall official after
providing much of the information on which the report was to be
written. The report was formal and went through the committee
decisions, reports of officers and correspondence and added nothing
to what Ferguson and the present writer had told Councillor
Oldfield and the town-hall officials.

By this time Ferguson had already interviewed the chief actors in
the drama, except for the Simons who declined to say anything, and

a short news feature film appeared in which the main points of the town clerk's report were covered. In addition, a valuation of the land with planning permission was put at £30,000 and the question was asked whether in fact Thomas Simon Builders Ltd had cleared the £20,000 profit which it seemed had been made. The film report made no attempt to accuse Simon of any illegal act, or even of bad faith, but did make it clear that some questions still needed to be asked.

The two Simon brothers acted swiftly and issued a writ for libel, and there the matter ended for the time being at least. Unfortunately, however, the Marlborough Drive group still felt cheated. None of them had known that the film was to be shown on the particular night that it appeared and none involved had seen it. When they asked if they might see a recording at the studios, Ferguson, who would gladly have done so, had to decline on the advice of the company solicitors because the matter was now *sub judice*.

Another incident from a council's activities in a district with its own newspaper depicts further the way in which reality is constructed by the press from a conflicting set of versions. It concerns the activities of Charles Brown, an estate agent councillor in Subville and the Subville Tenants Action Group. The Subville Tenants Action Group was formed to fight the activities of commercial landlords, and estate agents who bought up property in order to redevelop it as luxury flats and offices. One of the sources of their concern and target of their attacks was the Subville Housing Association, a non-profit-making body which provided cost rent accommodation for tenants who became members of the association. The action group noted that the people who moved into the flats were relatively well-to-do, paid rents that the action group members could not afford and that the office to which tenants applied for was that of the estate agent and Councillor Charles Brown. They also noted that the erecting of the flats was undertaken by a builder who was also a councillor, Bill Tugg.

The action group had instituted their own newspaper, the *Subville Free Press*. One of the volunteer writers, a student called Bill Tate, wrote an article on the business activities of councillors listing the companies and businesses in which they had interests. He had got most of this information from the Registry of Companies in Company House, London, via some members of the Labour Party's full-time research staff. In addition he had accused Brown and Tugg of obtaining fees for their work as committee members of the Subville Housing Association and half a dozen other such organizations operating from Brown's estate agents' office. This was not true, and the *Free Press* in their next issue had to publish a full retraction both of this allegation and any implication that Brown and Tugg were in the housing association or using their positions as councillors for what they could get out of it.

Tate had failed to understand that housing associations are a means by which groups of people can rent property at cost rent, or buy their homes collectively as an alternative to owner occupation, which perhaps they cannot afford, or to being a council tenant, which perhaps they do not desire or for which they would only qualify after many years on a waiting-list. As such they provide no direct source of revenue to those professional people who frequently start them before handing over control to the tenants. But they can and do generate fees for architects, surveyors and estate agents who are often appointed on an indefinite basis as 'managing agents'. It may well be that they also enable builders to win contracts. The Cohen Committee, which was set up by the government to inquire into the operation of voluntary housing associations, recognized this and accepted that it was desirable that professional people should be attracted to these bodies in order to avoid the chaos which often results from amateur forays into the field of finance. In return, it was considered quite legitimate that such professionals should take their normal fees. Thus one might make out a case that an individual was benefiting from his participation in a housing association. But it would not be directly for work done as a committee member; rather it would be for professional service or as a result of building contracts. Such benefits, however, would neither be of necessity illegal or clandestine or even questionable.

However, another complication gave rise to more activity within Subville Council. After the *Free Press* had closed down as a result of having to pay the expenses of Brown's and Tugg's lawyers, another member of the council, Alex Allison, said that he was disturbed by the fact that some members of the council, who were also members of housing associations and businessmen, might be seen to have a clash of interests when these housing associations co-operated with the council on certain housing projects. He also wanted to know whether it was true that some council housebuilding sites had been passed over to the associations, and that in some cases work which was funded out of grants from the local authority and the central government was being undertaken by council members' building firms without being put out to public tender.

The *Subville Weekly Examiner* carried a report based entirely on what Allison had said in the council and the reply by those opposed to his view, who had accused him of mud-slinging. The *Examiner* also ran an editorial leader denying any allegation of specific bad faith or corruption, but calling for a compulsory register of councillors' interests in order to allay any possible rumours and to protect the good name of the council and local government. The *Midnorth Gazette* reporter who was at the meeting did not cover the debate and the Longtown News Services reporter sent in a report to *The Guardian* and the *Telegraph* stating that Subville Council would spend over £2 million on housing schemes in conjunction with housing associations in the borough. This story came from the minutes before the meeting and nothing from the debate was included in the story.

As a result of the debate a report was prepared by the town clerk. It explained that the council had a number of joint schemes with local housing associations for the provision of houses for those in need. Some of the schemes were with Shelter-type organizations for the homeless; others were with housing associations which were not primarily geared for the needy but for people who did not fit into the normal owner-occupier or council tenant categories. In order to gain council co-operation a given percentage of the tenancies had to go to people on the council housing waiting-list. Where the old and the needy or the handicapped were provided with homes the schemes qualified for various grants, and all housing society or housing association schemes could be financed by mortgages from the local authority, the Housing Corporation (a government body) or the building societies with similar tax concessions to those available to individual owner-occupiers. In some cases, the report stated, contracts were awarded to firms without being put out to tender where such firms had already won contracts for similar work, and the procedures for this were laid down in appropriate legislation.

In the debate which ensued, Councillor Allison and those opposed to the policy, especially the release of council house building sites, reiterated their arguments that it was undesirable for any councillor to be in the position of having conflicts of interest, while the supporters of the policy accused them of innuendo. The *Subville Weekly Examiner* carried a report of the debate and included that part of the town clerk's report explaining the generalities of the policy of co-operation with the voluntary housing bodies. The *Midnorth Gazette* referred briefly to the report, concentrating on the nature of the policy and on a statement of the figures involved. The report of the debate suggested that there had been a disagreement about whether the policy was desirable or not, but it gave no indication of any reasons for the disagreement. Longtown News Services did not bother to cover the issue, apparently on the grounds that it was only a re-run of the previous story.

Even the readers of the *Subville Weekly Examiner*, which again called for a strict register of councillors' interests, would have gleaned no specific information about councillors' business activities, or any details which would have enabled them to judge whether there really was a conflict between 'public' duty and private interest, and if this was the innuendo, whether or not it was well founded. Yet in the town clerk's report there was a statistical and financial appendix, which was published, showing that Tugg's building firm had had over half a million pounds' worth of contracts through the Subville Housing Association and others run from the same address, that of Brown's estate agency. This work had also been contracted without being put out to tender. Another contract involved a piece of land which had been released by the council's housing committee. And the Subville Housing Association and others run from Brown's offices had a further half-dozen schemes, some of which were capable of attracting government grants and some for which Tugg's firm was to do the work, all in the pipeline. Altogether the work involved over £1 million. All of the schemes were recorded as being managed by Brown's estate agency, while the estimates of annual management fees for each housing unit printed in the report, which would have involved a total sum of around £4,000, would have provided a continuing source of income to the agency.

At every stage Brown and Tugg had behaved with scrupulous legality and honesty. They had always declared an interest and had never attempted to hide their business activities which were in any event quite legal and proper, in terms of the legal framework of business and local government. What was being questioned both in the council and in the pages of the *Subville Weekly Examiner* was the desirability of that framework.

What were the restraints which were generated in this case? It was not a question of there being a total blanket on the coverage of events but of a construction of those events into a generalized account of an argument without any of the data on which the generalized conclusions might be based. Once again a group calling into question the good faith of the exponents of the governmental system was in conflict with the consensus framework, represented both by the press and the local government structure. In a sense it achieved one of its objectives, since there was an inquiry into the issue of contracts involving councillors, but the whole debate was conducted in public without reference to specifics. The members of the group felt they had been crushed by the Defamation Act and their own lack of money. To the local officials and the councillors involved they were troublemakers and extremists, or at best misguided idealists. There was an irremediable clash of ideology. But if there was an official report with undisputed references to councillors' business activities, which by common consent were certainly not criminal or wicked, and either desirable and wise, or not, according to belief, why did councillors and the established press not mention the councillors concerned by name in their debates and reports? And why indeed should it be necessary to rename them here, alter the town, transform the nature of the contracts, and doctor the actual figures involved?

The difficulty is twofold: the law of libel and its interpretation by the courts on the one hand, and popular uncertainty and fear of the law on the other. The existence of a report prepared by council officials would not in itself guarantee immunity from litigation, while council debates are not completely privileged in the way that House of Commons proceedings and reports of them are. The councillors in debates on the building contracts either accepted the general view that it was not proper to mention specific names or feared the consequences because of this uncertainty.

For the newspaper there is a much greater difficulty. A good 'scandal' story might result in a considerable increase in readers at best, especially if there was an expectation by the public that more would follow. But for a small weekly paper the penalty for such a story if it proved libellous might be damages which would obliterate ten years of profit. An independent paper would almost certainly close down, a chain paper would either close down itself or lose its editor and perhaps the reporter responsible. Additionally, and more typically (in the sense that such a case rarely arises but the fear of it conditions the editor's approach), the editor of a small paper has to make his own decisions. Even to take counsel's advice might mean forfeiting a week's profit in fees. Thus in terms of the mini-max story the potential costs more than outweigh the profit of a 'scandal' story, unless it is protected by being an account of a court proceedings against a specific councillor or official. This may well tend to create a picture of local government in which there are a majority of utterly worthy people and a 'small minority' who are double-dyed criminals, because the only detailed look at the other side of the local government personnel is when details such as the Poulson case, or the Birmingham architect's department case, or the case of the ex-Mayor of Manchester, who as a solicitor obtained a large legacy from a client, come into court. The ordinary, everyday, non-criminal events, in which conflicts of interest arise, appear to have no place for discussion.

Such fear on the part of editors and reporters is not entirely without foundation. Disclaimers in reports (or books) of the type stating that 'there is no suggestion that Councillor X was doing anything illegal or criminal' are insufficient protection against the claim that the imputation is that X was using his position to further his own advantage or the interests of his relatives. In such a case it is not enough to be able to prove, say, that the events, the award of contracts or the sale of land at a profit took place. It is necessary to show either that there was no defamatory imputation in the words, or that, if made, the imputation was based firmly on fact. The legal technicalities involved in establishing proof of an allegation are a matter for the specialist. But it does seem difficult to write about a councillor's business interests where they could be seen to conflict with his municipal activities without any detailed consideration of the facts being construed as libellous. The very fact of recording the events might even be taken as implying that something was wrong about them.

Conclusion

The argument in this chapter has been that the sort of free exchange of ideas which is associated with a free-market ideology implicit in a pluralist view of politics is not strictly speaking an analysis but, rather, an ideological view of events. Furthermore, the notion of the pressure group as an element generating this type of competition, the political party stabilizing it and the press providing the means by which ideas are exchanged and compete, is part of that ideological view. Versions of events which challenge this pluralist conception are excluded from the media of communication and from the political process as the result of a number of factors which are endemic in the structured nature of the social processes.

These factors are: the built-in dependence of the local press on the local authority as a source of regular news coverage which given individuals can cut off as a form of punishment; the need for speed in creating versions of events by local newspapers, which means that regular suppliers of information have power over the newspapermen that the supplier of one story or isolated pieces of information does not have; the endemic secrecy of local government, which, in the case of Councillor Simon's field, meant that none of the information available to the council officials was available to the press; the commercial nature of the newspaper enterprise, with the consequent reluctance of the editor to touch 'risky' material; and the libel laws. At the same time the isolation of the protest group with an anti-consensus grievance is conducive to the development of a 'conspiracy theory of history' approach which exacerbates the conflict with establishment sources of power and channels of protest. One such channel of protest is the 'official' pressure group whose success is dependent on its acceptability to the local authority, because it accepts the rules of the game of negotiations with a formal bureau-cratic structure and a mutual acceptance of the good faith and good sense of the other party. In just the same way as the conspiracy theorist fits each event into his conspiracy version, in which politicians are scoundrels and the press are 'in with them', the proponents and practitioners of consensus label all who see conspiracies as paranoid, extremists, or misguided. For a study in blind faith in an established system of government one should consider how long it took the 'experts' on the United States to accept the 'paranoid' Ellsberg McGovern accounts of Watergate, or other 'paranoid' versions of Chile or Vietnam, and also consider the fact that when a conspiracy is revealed in one field of government activity, there is a willingness to continue crediting the government with good faith in other areas, and that one immediate reaction is to brand anti-consensus protesters with anti-personnel words such as 'paranoids', 'extremists', 'malcontents' and 'communists'. This is not to argue that conspiracies or malign class interests explain unequivocally political conflict or the reticence of the press. As an explanation that is inadequate and unacceptable. But equally unacceptable is the theory that the liberal-democratic polity is a competition between groups which spring up to represent whatever legitimate interests there are, with the government as an impartially benevolent referee. Either view of events is ideological and depends for its survival upon the same circulatory process of validation.

4
Respectable protest

In this chapter the characteristics of 'respectable' protest will be considered. It is not claimed that this account universally characterizes the nature of normal pressure group and protest group activity on local government. What does seem evident is that there are cogent reasons why successful protests achieved a coverage and recognition denied by the nature of the political-journalistic system to those referred to in the previous chapter. These reasons may constitute a generalizable explanation of such political phenomena. But no claim is made for 'scientifically' unassailable explanations nor for 'scientific' tests of propositions. Such claims usually rest in the social sciences on the preposterous notions that questionnaires constitute actual evidence of behaviour; that responses to such questionnaires about perceptions of events, reasons for actions, attitudes etc., can be quantified; that these quantifications can be correlated in terms of measured probabilities often involving several places of decimals; that actors have qualities known as 'attitudes' which are stable and that these are in some kind of definitive and definable relationship with action. Further, as Cicourel and others[1] have shown, the exercise is done within the context of a theoretical scheme which predetermines the structure of the questionnaire and therefore selects areas of relevance for the actors involved and does not rely on their own perception of events as a source of explanation. This position in the end presupposes that actors do not know why they do things and that social scientists do.

All such scientific positions should be rejected for the reason that the so-called expertise of social scientists is based either on language or a system of numbers or notation which is a shorthand for language. Words are in principle not reducible to a level of certainty where their meanings are not disputed. Second, words are not constructs for describing reality but are the means by which we construct reality, so that the ambiguity is not simply in the mode of analysis or the criteria of measurement but also bedded in the subject matter of the problems we attempt to solve. Third, the social 'facts' of belief systems – norms, values, anomie, alienation, class consciousness, group solidarity etc. – are, wholly or in part, internal mental phenomena of individuals, which are (a) not directly observable and (b) expressed *only* in words. (An action does not express a mental state at the level of abstraction of 'anomie' or 'norm', since the same action may be explicable in terms of various norms; and a given norm may be used to justify a variety of actions. 'Reaction formation', of the Mertonian-type explanation of apathy, excessively zealous obedience and rebelliousness as symptoms of the same cause, provides a vivid example.)[2] The aim of generalizable explanations here is to attempt an understanding of how the different elements in social relationships are related and how actors play their parts in various social processes. Rather than attempting to offer an overall correlation between categories such as social class and political efficacy from which an analysis of particular social processes can be adduced, let us begin from the premiss that an analysis which will not explain one instance will not explain any; while an explanation of the detailed relationships of one instance is at least capable, in principle, of explaining others.

Respectability, the press and government

'Respectability' in the local political arena is conferred by the press, the other media and government agencies – especially the local authorities. The organizers of pressure groups often believe that by gaining publicity, usually in the press, they will be helped to gain access to the local authority. The cases examined in this book suggest that such a belief inverts the order of the genesis of recognition. The press tended in these cases to follow the local authority in the sense that this was the chief source of news, and conflicts with the local authority had either to be mentioned in the minutes or at least involve some action taken towards the local authority before coverage was conferred. Even those incidents where campaigns were instigated or supported by the newspaper began as a result of local government action or as a result of information officially provided by local government. The course of the press coverage also followed very closely the course of events in the local government set-up.

It is perhaps helpful to distinguish 'protest' and 'pressure groups'. What is meant by pressure groups in this context is an organized, relatively cohesive collectivity engaged in activities calculated on the part of its officials and members to influence local government or central government policy. Protest, on the other hand, refers to the activity of complaining about and attempting to alter a particular aspect of government or government policy. Now it may be that a pressure group will concentrate entirely on the achievement of one political objective; it is associated with one identifiable protest. At the other pole pressure groups such as the Chamber of Trade, in its relationships with government at any given time, may be involved in any number of specific issues or none. In pressure groups set up to prosecute one protest, one may find that others are brought to them as an umbrella organization or that the pursuit of the major protest itself develops into a multitude of other issues. Thus it may be possible that a first step by the organizers of a protest is to attach their protest to an already established and preferably sympathetic pressure group and capitalize on the ongoing relationships between the groups' officials and council officials, the press etc.

Acknowledgement by the local authority of a pressure group may take a number of forms. The pressure group may become part of a recognized, institutionalized conflict-regulating, 'collective bargaining' situation. In this event the pressure group officials negotiate on a formal basis with the officials of the local authority into whose bureaucratic structures of action, linguistic style, expertise and secrecy they are drawn. Alternatively it may gain recognition by the party political stratum of the local government system, with public meetings addressed by councillors and meetings by officials with councillors in the hope of gaining their advocacy in council and committee meetings. Third, it may involve the use of statutory or common law rights of protest and resistance which the council has no power to prevent or control. The most common form of such protest and resistance is the Department of the Environment's local public inquiry into objections about corporation planning decisions or road projects. Plainly when we refer to local authority recognition the words are used literally; it does not imply an approval of the pressure group or its policies.

In the local authority the pressure group officials are dealing with a complex bureaucracy in which the appearance of rigidity is a tactic employed from time to time as part of a survival-cum-imperial strategy by individuals which disguises a social and organizational situation of change and competition. Change comes from two main sources and can be further broken down in terms of its effects: (a) the resolution of contradictions and competition within the bureaucracy itself and (b) the implementation (or avoidance) of change by central government. It is useful to divide the changes so wrought in terms of (a) changes in the structure of the organizational blueprint and (b) changes in the policies implemented through this bureaucratic formation. It is accepted that such a distinction is not an exact replication of reality, in that changes in policy mean *effective* if not legal changes in the power balance and therefore in the bureaucracy; and that the bureaucratic blueprint expresses itself as a resource formation employed by actors in behaviour and that behaviour is the execution of policy.

The endemic changes in the local authority stem both from the political control and from the nature of the occupations of the bureaucracy. Patently, in areas of fairly even political balance, competition between different political parties for control of the council leads to changes in policy; in terms of comprehensive education, the extent of council-house building; direct works departments; ventures by councils into municipalization of the local economy. Even in local 'one-party-states' such as in the agricultural shires or the mining areas of the north-east, Yorkshire or South Lancashire, internal divisions in the parties over ideology and personalities can lead to changes in policy. The occupations in which the local authority are engaged relate to progressive bodies of professional expertise and are intended to solve problems of a changing society. Town planning, for instance, as a body of know-ledge is progressive in the sense that it takes in new ideas, moves into new areas. It has to take account of new fashions and new evidence – about the influence of motorways or factory siting; about the effects of high-rise flats on social conditions. Education has had to take account since the war of a vast expansion in adult education. In all departments, as well as qualitative changes in policies, there are quantitative changes in the number of employees. At all levels the numbers of government employees has risen and continues to rise.[3]

A corollary of these changes in policy and scale of operations has been a change in bureaucratic formations. New management tech-niques have been made necessary. In the area of education, for instance, further education area organizers take on more administra-tion and bargain with the central education office for resources. In secondary education the increased size of schools and the career structure of teachers have led to the creation of more specifically administrative roles; graded posts are awarded more to non-class-room teachers. Within certain departments divisions of labour begin to manifest themselves. Within the Public Health Department there is a division of labour between the inspectorate administering the housing laws and those engaged in the inspection of things relating to hygiene. Within the town clerk's department management functions become separated from legal functions so that different deputy town clerks may be administering what are effectively differ-ent departments. In some larger, more 'progressive' authorities the primacy of the legal department is surrendered to a managerial department, which in turn is reflected in changes in the committees structure, a policy or finance and general purpose committee taking on the tasks of the supervision of purely managerial roles with a separate legal committee. Managerialism may also express itself in the development of a formal committee system operating among the chief officers of various corporation departments in which policy proposals are made for submission to the party political stratum, at which decisions of the council and committees are considered in terms of requisite administrative action and at which sub-political decisions, those reserved to officers, are discussed. Increasingly decisions which used to be taken by elected representatives, and which are regarded as 'detail', have been delegated to full-time officers.

Additionally physical, the technological factors generate changes of policy and administrative arrangements. Expansion of departments often means the removal of some departments into new buildings, which carries implications both for the demands of internal communications and surveillance and for the relative power of heads of departments removed from the central control of the bureaucracy. A head of a department with guaranteed income and powers, such as an education officer, can reasonably hope to run a separated education department with an increased degree of autonomy. A department which is newly fledged and widely regarded with suspicion such as, say, a new social services department, might of course find that offices away from the main town hall will only underline its isolation and powerlessness and remove its chief officers from influential ears and powerful levers. On the other hand the introduction of a computer into the local authority is likely to involve a number of consequences related to the general organizational effects of technological innovation[4] which are manifested in industrial settings. Heads of departments bent on organizational imperialism may attempt to gain control of the computer, either for the satisfaction of their own technical needs or alternatively as an extension of managerial control. Smaller local authorities without the resources to afford, or the workload to necessitate a computer of their own, may set up regional computer centres which are jointly administered which in turn presupposes both internal and external changes in the bureaucracies of the councils involved.

Changes may also occur as a result of pressures and direct ukases from central government. These may take the form of direct statutory alterations to the structure of local government undertakings such as the setting up of regional transport executives or to the nature of local government of itself, such as the local government reorganization acts. These changes, although obviously undertaken with certain general policy objectives in view, have an initial effect which is primarily organizational. Indeed there is some reason to believe that at least in the short term the effect of such moves as amalgamation of local authorities produces not the consummation devoutly desired, an increase in administrative productivity, but the opposite, an increase in the number of administrators. This may be an effect which is overcome as change works through the system or it may be part of a process of organizational imperialism; as organizations expand in size, they increase their areas of activity internally and externally at a more than proportionate rate. There are, on the other hand, changes wrought primarily from the effect of central government which are primarily related to the achievement of specific policy changes. The classic *modus operandi* is the issue of ministry circulars to local government offices. Officials inform councillors about the circulars and give their interpretation of them at committee meetings. These are undoubtedly a considerable weapon in the hands of an officer, who will have clip folders filled with them and other ministerial missives. They may be quoted to show that given policies can or cannot be carried out. They may involve the introduction of comprehensive education or the implementation of housing acts.

The purpose of this digression is to underline these two points: (a) that local government is not a static structure of role relationships which can be understood by examining the legal functions of officers and departments but an arena of competing interests involving constant flux and (b) that different officers, and councillors, have and pursue different interests, such as the defence of their jobs or departments or expansion of their powers. The result is that organizational work involves the maintenance or achievement of viability as a competitor. And the mode of execution of administratively defined procedures is a stratagem in a campaign. Standard textbooks on local government appear to regard the system as static, with change as a movement from one static state to another.[5]

The final element in the triad is the local newspaper. The notion given credence by many American studies of the press,[6] that newsmen have criteria of what constitutes news and which they apply to items of news, is an irrelevant reconstruction of newspaper activity to make it fit the assumptions of rationality and causality of social science. Items of news are not 'facts' *sui generis* but constructions of reality arising out of the activity of news creation. This activity, moreover, is not totally accounted for by the notion of actors' applying criteria of selection to individual news items. The 'good' story is not simply an evaluation based upon the content of the story but relates to organizational factors, the journalists' perceptions of markets and of the audience. When one refers to a good story and enumerates its qualities as A, B and C, this is not to say that an editor measures each news item against them or that a reporter has them in mind when assessing incidents suitable for construction. It is simply a way of evaluating and describing the good story in relation to its social context, an attempt to provide part of an explanation of how a journalist goes about the business of being a journalist.

Good stories vary according to context. If a reporter is selling a story on a lineage basis he will write a different good story for the

Daily Mirror than for *The Guardian* or the *Telegraph*. One ex-colleague of mine who began his career as a local journalist and 'stringer'* in the 1930s, subsequently moving to the *Daily Graphic*, was much distressed by his short experience later as a night sub on *The Guardian*. The chief cause of his distress was that stories about immigrant knife fights were turned down in favour of accounts of Arts Council grants being made to various groups of worthies. His notions of good stories were gained in a different milieu from the genteel offices of *The Guardian*. An editor works with a picture of his audience in mind; it is a structured hypothesis which he applies to his work as a journalist-cum-organizer but whose standards of proof or disproof are hard to assess. It could be that in this case the old campaigner's preoccupation with knife-waving Pakistanis was a good guide to gaining readership. Let us look at the audiences which various newspapermen aim at and examine later the conclusions they draw about the suitability of stories.

The Guardian, for instance, in its northern editorial home news coverage, attempts to throw off any vestiges of parochialism which may have clung to it since it carried the word Manchester in its masthead. Local government coverage of the Manchester area has to have a more general relevance than simply being a story about Manchester. The audience in mind is a wider, national, or at least regional one. A story must therefore have some general theme such as individual rights or relate to some nationally relevant story or issue – a government white paper on urban renewal, for example, or a national growth of interest in, say, conservation. On a more local scale (though not a smaller scale in terms of circulation) the *Manchester Evening News* will have no truck with the parish-pump approach either. The editor aims at creating a paper which caters for a regional, conurbation-wide readership. A Withington† story or a Stretford† story therefore has also to be at least a Manchester, preferably a north-west and possibly a national story. Somewhere between the two, the *Daily Telegraph* provides through the use of freelance agencies a local news coverage of the whole country on a regional basis. In a sense it is aimed at a national middle-class readership and also at local readerships. Short local stories from local freelances about the affairs of various town councils have been a feature of the *Daily Telegraph*, which in turn sensitizes local journalists to the fact that if they have a local story to sell, the *Telegraph* is a likely customer. This stress on the influence of the editor's perception of his audience is not to belittle what has already been said about the passivity of the press and its relationship to perceived

*A 'stringer' is a journalist who works an area as a freelance for the nationals and evenings.

†Manchester suburban areas.

market forces; plainly the audience constitutes one of the relevant markets for newspapermen.

To illustrate the process indicated above, it is necessary to outline briefly the history of a number of pressure groups and their relations both with the press and with the local authority.

A 'constitutional' protest

In this case a village at the centre of a fashionable suburb, Garden Meadows, was threatened with extinction to make way for a new precinct. Around 300 houses were to be demolished to make way for an increased number of shops, new offices and the attendant car park. The council put its plans with a model on display in the local library. Officials answered questions of visitors and a public meeting was held to hear queries and suggestions. One old resident of the area, Gwenda Churchill, a publican's widow of small stature but terrible ferocity, went into the back room of the library and found some other maps which showed a much wider area of demolition to be carried out later with the development of a new road – which was not included in the PR display of the shopping centre. An official attempted to make her leave. Whereupon she pointed out that she had withstood Hitler's bombs and being English would fight for her 'little bit of England'. If she wasn't frightened of Hitler she certainly wasn't frightened of him.

At the meeting a packed audience, some of whom had to be accommodated outside the hall, heard Gwenda repeat her analogy between the war and their present crisis and her allegations that the council planned much wider demolition of houses eventually than had been revealed. Many of the questions related to individual concern about compensation and rehousing, but a number of people raised fundamental questions about the desirability of more shops and offices in a residential area and about the desirability of destroying houses to make way for car parks. An economist raised the issue of the viability of the scheme as an economic proposition.

The meeting was called by the council as the brainchild of the planning department which wanted to extend public participation. But what the department was interested in was questions and suggestions. The planning officer's report to the subsequent planning committee meeting reflected for one reason or another an unwillingness to acknowledge the fundamental nature of many of the objections. It referred instead to the smaller detailed issues which were raised.

The meeting turned out to be effective in engendering public participation in a way which was not intended, however. As a result of the uproar at the meeting, which went unreported in the press, a number of the locals met afterwards and decided to call a meeting of residents to defend Garden Meadows.

This was done, and a local shopkeeper, Reginald Beddows, was elected chairman. Chairmanship was not one of Mr Beddow's apparent talents. A level of suburban anarchy attended his efforts, chiefly consisting of the airing by various members of pet aversions or recurrent anxieties not necessarily related to the utterances of other members of the meeting. Out of the meeting, however, they decided to form a Garden Meadows Society to fight the council proposals. At Mr Beddows's suggestion they agreed they should have a legal constitution drawn up. The compelling reasons for this which won approval were (a) it would give the society a legal official status on which to base its credibility in negotiations and requests for information from the council and (b) it would be necessary to put fund raising etc. on a firm footing.

As a result of the chaos attending Mr Beddows's chairmanship a number of members who were not previously known to one another as a group suggested that Jack Webb, an economist, should stand as chairman against Beddows. Although a relative newcomer Webb had distinguished himself by his articulate and measured criticism at the meeting. Further, there was throughout the course of the subsequent campaign a widespread suspicion of the shopkeeper's motives. Webb was elected chairman.

The management committee also included: George Reeves, a housing manager for a charitable housing society and a socialist; Martin Wild, a university lecturer who was a member of the same ward Labour Party as Reeves; Bridget Cooney, another Labour Party member who was also a lecturer; Ted Pugh, an artisan, and an old friend of Webb. Carol Land, who was a member of Garden Meadows Community Association, became secretary. Gwenda Churchill was also a member and so were Beddows, Fred Holmes, an ex-Liberal councillor, Ron Trapp, a Liberal Party member and architect, and a number of residents who were involved in collecting funds. The size of the committee varied with co-options and resignations. To an extent, anyone who wanted to come could do so, provided they had some suggestion to offer or a service to provide. People left the committee as their interest waned or when they left the district.

Their conflict with the council went through a number of stages, at some of which they put great value on getting publicity, at others on not getting it, while at others they were indifferent. At the outset they wished to challenge the council's proposal. They had to challenge two matters: first, the council's plan for the area's redevelopment; second, the survey by the health department which preceded this plan's implementation and which would (almost certainly) declare unfit the working-class houses at the centre of the Garden Meadows suburb. The only member of the management committee who was both articulate and an inhabitant of one of these houses was Gwenda Churchill. There were other members of the committee who came from the houses who were active as collectors and distributors but tended not to participate in decision-making. Their comments tended to be complaints about failures of organization, or suggestions about alternatives to methods of operation.

We shall look at the campaign in three stages: the campaign of opposition to the clearance policy; the proposition of an alternative plan and a referendum; negotiation and the public inquiry.

From the outset the Garden Meadowites wanted to oppose the council's proposals. At the beginning this took the form of opposition in various forms with the one common factor of crude opposition to anything which might alter the nature of the area. At the public meetings many of the speeches were about holes in the council's logic in wanting to knock down houses; or were accusations of corruption or bad faith. Less was said about alternative schemes. At this stage George Reeves was an organizational keystone. He knew how the council would go about the health survey and what defects they would look for; he was familiar with the housing acts under which surveys would be conducted.

Partly at the instigation of Reeves and partly using the experience of other protest groups, which they had gleaned both from the press and from personal contact, the committee decided to carry out their own survey of housing in Garden Meadows. Reeves's expertise was also crucial in formulating their support for a policy of general improvement as an alternative to demolition. He was conversant with the 1969 Housing Act proposals for general improvement areas. The survey also included questions which would enable them to assess the viability of the affected streets as a general improvement area under the act.

Finally, by this time there had been an exchange of letters between the society and the council officials, which prompted a further kind of survey. The council letters denied the existence of any cut-and-dried clearance proposals, and questioned the extent to which a general opposition to the scheme actually existed. This last point could be challenged by direct survey evidence about who did and who did not want to move out. The committee therefore decided to carry out a social survey of the people who wanted to go and who wanted to stay. Additionally, in order to show the area as a viable community in terms acceptable under the legislation, they included questions about duration of residence and relatives living within the area.

To manage the operations of the society a system of functional sub-committees was set up which reported back to the management committee. Some of the sub-committees, such as that dealing with relations with the town hall, carried out their own operations. The committee dealing with the implementation of the survey had to operate teams of workers at street level. Thus the society was operating a bureaucratic system which conflicted in aims with that of the local government bureaucracy but at the same time derived its functional criteria either from the activities of local government or from an identical set of legal rules (the housing acts).

This stage of the campaign was conducted as a result of discussions in the management committee, at which a dominant role was played by Reeves, Wild and Webb. The main inspiration was Reeves, whose keen interest and professionalism gave him the advantage in discussion in that he had the clearest idea about what was to be done.

However, the implementation of a GIA required two other conditions to be fulfilled. First, it was necessary to demonstrate that a viable majority of people in the area wished to participate; secondly, to proffer a plan of such an area after improvement. Wild proposed that the society should conduct a referendum of everyone in Garden Meadows – with its electoral roll of 20,000. A referendum of those in the immediate area of the proposed demolition would not do – an improved housing *and shopping centre* would need the support of all those in the catchment-area of the shops.

At the same time the hour was fast approaching when the health committee was going to consider its inspectors' report. Some kind of opposition to this was needed. Webb stressed the need for politicking among councillors, especially Labour members – since they were the controlling group – who were opposed to GIAs as an alternative to demolition. A number of members raised objections to the total concentration of activity on a referendum at the expense of everything else. But Wild argued that a referendum might well change the course of the health committee vote in the face of a massive opposition to demolition. After an impassioned plea from Wild, invoking the principles of participatory democracy, a general meeting supported in principle the holding of a referendum. At Wild's suggestion a referendum committee was formed which was to meet as regularly as was necessary and report back to the management committee. At the inaugural meeting of the referendum committee Wild appeared with a document combining a flow chart and an organizational chart showing the breakdown of the committee into functional sub-committees dealing with areas such as the mobile exhibition, compilation of plans, dealings with the press and so on.

When it came to discussion of who was to be in charge of dealings with the press, Wild made it plain that he wished to take on this role. On the other hand Ron Trapp the architect said that he had quite a 'lot of friends' in the press and television. But when it was pointed out to Ron Trapp that his expertise would be much needed and was without substitute in the vital matter of creating a new plan, he did not press the point. There ensued a discussion on the tactics to be employed in tackling the press – especially in view of a request from the *Manchester Evening News* to Webb that evening for information. This was their first contact with the news media and was the result of a tip-off by an association member to the *Manchester Evening News*.

Wild wanted to control the flow of news in order that it should have an impact, rather than merely dribble. He had the idea of 'selling' stories by angling them in a newsy light, and press releases were to be put out with this in mind. However, the categories to which he referred in formulating his selling angle were abstract and ideologically in an unfamiliar vein to the newspaperman. He wanted to announce the opening of the campaign as a first time that people had taken matters into their own hands; as planning by participatory democracy; as an experiment in mobilization of the people. Now, while professional journalists also wanted stories with *angles* transcending the merely local, they did not opt for such categories. Their categories were less abstract and were ideological at a level which, they figured, was familiar to their readers: one man against the bureaucratic menace; OAPs fight for the environment. Nevertheless, Wild was striving to formulate handouts for the press that would at least meet with his conception of the sort of demands which were on the journalist.

The day of making a statement to the press was suggested as a Friday. It was pointed out that this was a bad day because it was too late to get in the northern editions of the dailies until Saturday and could only get in Friday's evening paper. Thursday afternoon would still get them in the Friday evening paper and in the Friday morning dailies. Wednesday would be better still. This is because Saturday is a 'small paper' day generally, whereas Thursday and Friday are generally big paper days because of the weight of advertisements. If you hold your news conference on Wednesday, taking deadlines into account, you maximize your chance of filling a gap in a 'big paper' day. A number of committee members soon caught on to this simple principle. Wild worked to this timetable.

Webb also appreciated the need, in making statements to the press, of being unambiguous and employing simple constructions. One of the members from the council estate, on the other hand, was still thinking in terms of writing letters to the correspondence column. At the management committee meeting various suggestions were put forward, varying from placing an advertisement in the *Evening News* to vague suggestions that they should somehow 'get the papers' to editorialize on behalf of the society. Another member, Mrs Siddon, had heard from an ex-neighbour who was on the *Guardian* editorial staff that the paper 'was not interested in local stories'. Another lady said she had heard the same about the *Manchester Evening News*.

Wild proceeded, however, to produce a flow of contacts. He already knew a reporter on the *Evening News* from his student days and members of Granada staff. He got in touch with Tattersalls news agency which supplied the *Daily Telegraph*. Prior to the press campaign he had been thinking in terms of coverage by the *Daily Mirror* and the other tabloid nationals as well as the 'qualities'. In the event, only the *Manchester Evening News* turned up to the first press conference at which Webb acted as chief spokesman. The issue was later taken up by *The Guardian* and the *Telegraph*.

Predictably the angle the papers adopted was that of 'residents fight to save village'. No one took up Wild's hard-sell on participatory democracy. Further, whereas Wild regarded this as a generally significant event, a trail-blazing experiment which happened to be occurring in Garden Meadows, the editors and reporters regarded it and other stories as small bread-and-butter stuff which was basically local but with a general application. They followed the story through with advance notice stories on the lines of 'health committee to decide village's future today'. Ironically, what appealed was not its uniqueness – which was what Wild hoped for – but its topicality. A number of similar campaigns were already on the boil in Manchester and over the rest of the country. A series of articles in the *Sunday Times* had tackled the whole subject of the difference between making plans according to what people ought to want as opposed to what they actually said they wanted. It included in one article the suggestion which was a generally accepted 'truth' among protest groups that Manchester Council's planning policy on housing was dictated by the Health Department. So Garden Meadows for the papers was one part of a bigger picture.

When it was realized that the health committee would meet before the referendum was held, the management committee decided to send the committee a petition in order to get some impact. Each sheet was sellotaped to the next and the representatives of the societies carried the 30 feet of paper like a train up the town hall steps, in front of a rotund Granada film cameraman and a reporter who had been laid on by Wild in advance. They were accompanied by a reporter for Tattersalls who was covering the story for the *Telegraph*. They got news coverage on television of about a minute with a few seconds of film. The cameraman and the reporter agreed that there 'wasn't much in it' as they stood outside the town hall and stared with professional lack of wonder at the protesters.

In a sense this marked the beginning of the end of the public stage of the fight. The society had proved by this time that a conflict existed, and the council committee now made the decision to declare the houses unfit and call for their clearance by a CPO. At this point the committee members took a decision deliberately to suppress information they had.

The referendum was a week off. The referendum committee met in the evening after the health committee had met. They knew by a tip-off that the decision had gone against them, but they decided that nothing should be said to the membership about it because such news might be disastrous in that people would conclude that they had lost already and would not vote in the referendum. The committee decided that no one should speak to the press apart from Webb and that no mention should be made about the decision until after the referendum. In the event, there was an 11 per cent poll (in a referendum of nearly 20,000 electors), of whom an overwhelming majority were against demolition and wholesale redevelopment and in favour of a general improvement scheme. When members of the society attended the next council meeting to canvass for the health committee's report to be referred back, this coincided with a massive rent protest by council tenants and there was no coverage of the Garden Meadows endeavours.

After the referendum Wild gave up his active role in the society because of family pressures. The functional sub-committee system had ceased to operate, the referendum committee dissolved. Webb continued as chairman. He played on what had appeared to him to be the salient areas of possible change throughout: within the Labour group as the GIA legislation which was passed by a Labour government became acceptable; on the differences of approach between the planning department and the health department. In this he was helped by the knowledge which the society had from contacts both within the Labour Party, and through it the Labour group, and among those in the planning department who had helped with inside information about plans, documents and internal politics throughout the campaign. The latter were low-status employees with no long-term commitment to their careers with the town hall.

Webb attended a planning committee meeting where he spoke and met planning officers on a number of occasions. He also met public health officials. At these meetings discussions took place over what each side's attitude was to various principles of planning and public health, and to various streets and blocks in Garden Meadow village. There was compromise over a number of points. The council abandoned its scheme to allow part of the land to remain in private hands. The association came increasingly to accept the need to redevelop the area; the questions were increasingly those of detail. When the

public inquiry was held the property development company representative attacked the council for letting them down and published
the details of meetings between the company's representatives and
council officers of a number of years. None of this appeared in the
press.

In this campaign the pressure-group organizers developed a small-
scale bureaucracy to cope with the council bureaucracy; they even
became drawn into the need for secrecy because they were privy to
certain committee decisions which might have proved damaging.
Throughout, their relationship with the council was co-operative
as well as competitive. They also used the formal political party
system to attempt to gain their objectives. Interestingly, they used
the press on the basis of a number of assumptions about journalists'
behaviour which were wrong, but they gained publicity because (a)
their active cultivation of the press made coverage of the story a
straightforward affair for the papers and (b) because their story
was topical (for totally different reasons from those stressed by their
press officer) and would therefore appeal to the hypothetical audiences of the newspapers concerned.

The logistics of high-speed protest

The case of a scheme to build council homes in two of Manchester's
largest parks provides an example of a campaign in which speed and
publicity were dominant considerations. Reliance on legally sanctioned rights of protest meant that negotiations with council departments were not necessary. In 1969 Manchester Corporation wanted
to build council homes on two major parks to the north-west and
north-east of the city: Heaton Park and Bogart Hole Clough. In
order to do this they used the device of the town meeting* in order
to gain the assent of the citizenry. But when the proposal appeared
in the *Manchester Evening News, Guardian* and *Telegraph* two
protest groups set themselves up: one was made up of the residents
near Heaton Park, the other of those in the less well-to-do area
around the smaller Bogart Hole Clough. One of the organizers of
the Bogart Hole Clough operation was a maintenance worker on a
national newspaper, and although he did not have a tame journalist
in tow he was able to use his acquaintance with reporters and aware-
ness of the ways of newspapers to find an appropriate reporter who
had inserted a small single-column story in the northern edition of
the *Daily Express* pointing out the existence of the protest group

*The town meeting is a right of public consultation in the constitution of
Manchester Corporation which is necessary for certain changes to be effected.
A final and overriding institution is the town poll, in which all voters have the
right to participate in the manner of a referendum.

and informing readers that the organizers were seeking members.

Many editors would regard such a story as a free puff which was losing the paper money for public announcements. Even though a given free puff would have involved no payment if refused as a story, such a story leads other readers to expect similar treatment and therefore threatens revenue. To get such a story in a national newspaper would be difficult for anyone without contacts in the newspaper industry. As a result of this story and others in the Manchester papers the two protest groups made contact and formed a common cause. The more well-to-do residents of the Heaton Park area were a valued source of funds. The two groups joined forces as the Parkland Action Group and engaged in a poster-and-leaflet campaign. Their activities were well covered by the press and local broadcasting. This was owing to a combination of factors: the issue was one raised in the corporation minutes; the pressure group had a good contact with journalists; and the story involved a multiplicity of good angles – individuals against bureaucracy, conservation of urban greenery, inter-party and intra-party conflict, with the bulk of the Labour Party supporting the 'official' council housebuilding policy and the majority of council opposition coming from Conservatives. At the same time rumours were floated around the Bogart Hole Clough area that the council was planning multi-storey flats, since the emotional appeal of such a possibility was much more powerful than, say, a small estate of OAPs bungalows. Reference was also made to the prefabs which had been built 'temporarily' in the area in the immediate post-war period but which had remained undisturbed long after exceeding their original life expectancy.

The Parkland Action Group organizers found out that when the town meeting had been a means of gaining support for council policy on previous occasions, it had not been particularly well attended. Indeed the council had not found it difficult to guarantee a majority for its policies on such occasions. The action group were already planning for the town poll, which they expected would follow their victory at the town meeting, before the meeting even took place. Popular opposition to the council building scheme was transported to the town hall by coach, and the supporters of the action group were so numerous that there was overspill from the one room appointed for the meeting of the citizens of Manchester (pop. 660,000). The protesters had an appointed speaker, refrained from lengthy argument, and the town meeting ended in defeat for the corporation. Such an event was big news for the *Manchester Evening News*, which had been given prior information about the mobile troops who were being brought in. They were photographed and filmed arriving at the meeting. Part of the success of this move depended on the council's not knowing of the Parkland Action Group's logistic

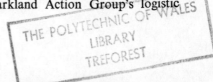

sophistication. This secrecy was aided by the fact that the group operated rather on the basis of a revolutionary cell or an electoral machine than as a public, bureaucratically organized, institutional pressure group. They had a clear objective to work to in a matter of weeks: victory at the town meeting. All their concerns were logistic and short-term, and protracted discussions were therefore out of the question. In the Bogart Hole section three organizers worked to produce the bulk of the popular support.

The campaign for the town poll attracted wide press coverage. It was, after all, a novel occurrence in which David clearly started out a clear favourite, having won the first bout with Goliath by a knock-out. In the poster campaign which was stepped up green paper was used to symbolize the greenery about to be nibbled by the municipal Frankenstein. Driving along in his Rolls-Royce, a local businessman, of great wealth and influence in the region and nationally, saw the posters and, being impressed by the energy and enterprise of the campaign, asked the organizers if they would call on him. This they did, explained their campaign and informed him that their major lack was finance. He asked them what they needed it for and they detailed a publicity campaign which they wished to mount, using a variety of techniques including full-sized advertising hoardings. The protesters stressed their professionalism and the need for money to engage the local authority in a businesslike way in the electoral battle. The businessman sympathized and gave them £700 on the understanding that the donation would remain anonymous.

In addition to the wide news coverage the campaign gained considerable coverage in the *Manchester Evening News* correspondence columns. As would be expected in a pressure-group campaign the letters were often inspired by the organizers who phoned supporters suggesting they wrote to the press. As well as using gossip-inspiration techniques and capitalizing on their inside knowledge of the newspaper industry, the campaigners called into play other social resources. A manager of a supermarket used his informal acquaintanceship with the manager of a publicity firm to gain concessions for the price of poster displays. He also distributed Parkland Action Group leaflets through women canvassers employed on advertising promotion campaigns for such items as washing powders.

The protesters reckoned on another advantage. First, that their support could be unified geographically among the residents of the areas near to the parks whose interests were directly affected. Against these relatively cohesive groupings, socially and geographically, the council's only interested supporters would be hopeful applicants on the waiting-list who might expect to be housed in those parts of the parks which were earmarked for the scheme. These would comprise a numerically small group. But more radically they were unknown, since no one was certain that given housing applicants would be housed in homes which were not yet built. Further, such people were not geographically cohesive and were members of socio-economic groups least likely to vote and hardest to organize politically. Established council-house dwellers might be seen as having an indirect interest in the issue, but since they were already housed it was not likely that they would have much motivation to participate. Second, the council would basically have to rely on solid Labour Party supporters who actually went along with the idea of using up part of the city's parks for house-building, while the opponents could rely on the support of those opposed to the scheme on political or aesthetic grounds as well of the numerous self-interested residents of the park districts. The protesters did not believe in any event that there would be much support among Labour supporters for such a crude, short-sighted and philistine proposal as the erosion of a primary working-class amenity for a comparatively small amount of housing land which could be got elsewhere. As it transpired, the poll on a small minority vote rejected the council proposal dramatically. The Parkland Action Group, having succeeded, ceased to exist.

One of the consequences for the organizers of the Bogart Hole Clough campaign was that when the council floated a rapid-transit scheme for crossing the city from south to north ending near to Bogart Hole Clough, some of the activists from the Parkland Action Group helped organize a joint opposition to the project. Once more 'action' was included in its title: this time it was the Manchester Civic Action Council. This, too, was apparently successful and employed many of the tried tactics of the Parkland Action Group. Newspaper and broadcasting coverage was maintained, letters to the editor were fired in barrages, a massed infantry attack was staged by middle-aged middle-class ladies on councillors at public meetings. Victory in the final event came in the form of a rejection of the scheme by the Ministry of Transport, which may well have been more the result of a report on the financial and operating calculations submitted through the action council by a mathematician whose home was likely to be affected, than owing to the epic pyrotechnics of the protest.

In this campaign, as in the Parkland campaign, after the issue became established as a viable story the organizers were periodically approached by the press, inquiring if they had any news. Their use of letter writing as a publicity technique may well have had unintended indirect consequences in the news coverage they received. Editors regard letters to the editor from readers as a source of news tip-offs, and an indication of the state of the audience's mind, as well as material for controversy in their correspondence columns.

Nonetheless, such letters need to be from their perceived readership and to relate to something which has some topicality as an issue. Newspaper offices very rapidly become sensitized to the style of nationally organized pressure groups. Local newspapers in, say, Manchester are not interested in typed letters from Ipswich about the need for the Common Market, from Leicester about the greatness of the British race, or from Aylesbury about the excessive power of the trade unions. But where the issue is relevant to a happening – the closure of a mill, a new development scheme, an influx of immigrants – which is clearly significant for the editor's perception of his readership, the letter provides information about the audience and affects his judgements about the coverage of news.

The respectable protest gains its respectability both from the nature of the issue it presents and from the social resources of the organizers of the protest. As to the nature of the issue, we are clearly not concerned with the inherent transcendental essence of the arguments but with its qualities as constructed and presented both by the protesters, government agencies and the communications media. The social resources of the organizers cover a variety of relevant skills, both particular to given social contexts and those general to differing situations. They may be 'structural' variables relating to membership of an organization or of an informal gossip-network. They may equally manifest them as ideological resources. Respectability of protest depends on its acceptability both to government and to the established media. The generation of this acceptability is the outcome of an interrelationship of factors which will be examined more closely after looking at the office organization of weekly newspapers in order to understand more fully the social construction of news.

PART THREE

The organization of local news

5

The *Littletown Independent*

In order to comprehend further the processes which go into the manufacture of news we shall study the relationships between ownership, organizational structure, personal interaction within the newspaper and relations between staff and outsiders, in two weekly newspaper offices in the north of England. In this chapter we shall deal with the *Littletown Independent*, a small family-owned paper operating in a rural market-town physically distinct from its neighbouring conurbations although serving as a peripheral dormitory for two such areas. In the next chapter we shall look at the *Blackville Examiner*, one of the largest local weekly newspapers in the country, part of a chain and serving a middle-sized traditional industrial area.

The *Littletown Independent* is owned by the Wright family. It was founded in the 1890s and espoused a parish-pump chauvinism from the outset. Its commitment was to Littletown and its interests: not to one or other of the two political parties as had been its dozen or so predecessors during the previous fifty years. The business had been run first by its founder, Soames Wright, and then jointly until the mid-1960s by his two sons – Harold, who managed the jobbing printing part of the enterprise, and Reginald, who had been editor. But then Reginald gave up the editorship to his deputy, Charles Debrett, continuing to come into the *Independent* offices on a part-time basis to write his weekly column. And Harold, who had spent many years wrangling with Reginald, because he thought that the printing business should have precedence over the newspaper business, died. Reginald in semi-retirement esconced himself in his private office above the shop front on Littletown High Street. He was physically isolated from his editorial staff as well as from the printing, compositing and photographic toilers. He hung over the premises like a disembodied presence: and when he wafted through the corridors like an ectoplasmic manifestation from a nineteenth-century *Punch* cartoon the staff passing him lowered their heads and uttered the words 'Morning Mr Reginald', to which his reply was a wordless grunt.

The shop front was all polished mahogany panels and frosted glass. Originally in the eighteenth and nineteenth centuries it had been a bookshop and printers, and it only ceased trading as stationers in the mid-1960s, and was still in business as a profitable, high quality jobbing printers. The offices to the rear were small and cramped, separated by hardboard partition walls. There was a file-room in which was preserved every edition of the *Independent* bound in leather-backed volumes since 1890-odd, in addition to local reference works and copies of local journals. The printing, compositing and photocopying workshops and dark-rooms were at the back of the offices; the printing machine-room being on the ground floor for dispatch, the others above.

The method of work and the power relations were both simple and complex; simple in the sense that they were relatively undifferentiated in a formal sense, but complex in their reliance on implicit understanding and lack of visibility to the naked, innocent eye. In attempting to assess organizational 'structure' we shall be concerned with working practices and the interaction between actors as ongoing processes. The notion of 'structure' as a reified abstraction is rejected. 'Structure' is used only as a shorthand for the understanding which the parties involved entertain about the regular aspects of the interactions; about power; about the negotiation of conflicting interests, about conflicting interpretations of reality.

The *Littletown Independent* had two district editions, the *Selford Independent* and the *Blacknoll Independent*. The organization of the office was geared to putting the three of them to bed on Wednesday, Thursday and Friday mornings. There was a 'Selford man' and a 'Blacknoll man' (a woman at the time) who wrote the stories which came in to their district offices. Afterwards they helped with the layout of their editions while the deputy editor, Jack Southall, worked with Debrett on layout at Littletown. Instead of simply running a main edition with different front and back pages and perhaps a 'slip' page inside for the different districts, Debrett altered the copy throughout the paper for different editions. This meant more work, more expense in printing and compositing costs, but resulted in three identifiably different papers appropriate to their own districts. The editor liked it that way, because it suited what he saw as the demands of the readers. Layout for Debrett had to meet three broad criteria.

(a) as much as possible should be fitted in;
(b) the material was readily available;
(c) that things were arranged where local people expected them.

The actual work of laying out the news stories and photographs on the layout sheets was done on a bench-top in a corridor through lack of space in the editor's or reporter's office. Debrett and Southall would be leaning over two working surfaces as others squeezed by. The process gave the impression of chaos; but it worked. They hardly ever finished late: their deadline was 11.00 a.m. and if they were behind it was only by a few minutes. 'I know some people [other journalists] might turn up their noses at the way we work here. It's probably more expensive, but it produces the kind of paper people want. It wouldn't win any layout competition – but the people in Littletown know the *Independent*. They don't care whether it wins layout competitions: what they want is local news in a form they understand and know,' Debrett explained. His attitude was that so long as the paper made a profit, even if costs were not kept to an absolute minimum and 'everybody was happy', there was no need to change.

Debrett was not the sole arbiter of what went into the paper, nor of its layout. Southall also had a say. Normally they discussed the rival merits of stories and a decision 'emerged' rather in the same manner as a new Conservative Party leader prior to the advent of party elections. But at times there was a disagreement, in which Southall had to accede. As an instance, Southall wanted to replace a story about 400 parents calling for a pedestrian crossing for their children to get to school with a story about a local 'with-it' wife of a vicar who collected fashion photographs. The photographer had provided a picture of the same cleric's lady wearing a skirt of non-ecclesiastical brevity and Southall thought this would 'brighten up' the front page – 'give it a bit of life'. No, said Debrett, the other was 'hard news' and more to the point, it involved 400 readers. About twenty children had been photographed crossing the road, under the tutelage of a warden and watched by a group of mothers. This was bound to sell papers. Southall accepted the decision without demure – in just the same way as Debrett accepted Southall's right to argue.

There were other limitations on Debrett's area of discretion. One was tradition: or rather a tradition which was seen by Debrett himself as limiting his choice. A potent illustration of this was that Littletown appeared from the paper to be in the process of becoming a ghost-town. It would certainly seem to the casual reader of the *Littletown Independent* that by far the most popular activity in the town was dying. This arose from the fact that the back page had been virtually institutionalized as a sort of journalistic charnel-house. This was the result of a regularized and predictable progress. The aged market-town cronies bought the paper and turned instantly to the deaths page to see whom they had outlived that week. Because they knew there was a deaths page they sent in obituaries of friends and family in the knowledge that they would be published more or less in full and without editorial amendment. In a sense then the back page was the prerogative and property of a section of readers – at least this was how Debrett saw it. And because he saw it in this way Debrett did not feel free to change the nature of the page.

Another part of the paper that was not entirely within the scope of the editor was Reginald Wright's weekly column. He could decide only within limits where it went. That is, it had to be on one of the inside news pages in a position of prominence. He could not relegate it to the bottom right-hand corner of the classified advertisements page or to the sports page. Further, although he could cut it to make it fit, he could not halve it or leave out part of it because he disagreed with it. He certainly could not drop it; the column was a proprietor's and ex-editor's privilege. But this did not trouble Debrett greatly. If the column contained an attack on a named local councillor (as it did at times) Debrett said he did not suffer much of a come-back.

Reginald, considered rather a queer customer by his staff, had been an army officer and came late into journalism. Although a member of the local *haute bourgeoisie* (inasmuch as there is one in Littletown) he kept himself aloof from the town and lived outside in a huge house, his out-of-work activities being concentrated on local history and the chairmanship of a local branch of a conservation society. This was a move specifically to avoid any possibility of pressure being brought on him by local interests. Lacking a son to take over the business, he had made Debrett and Southall members of the firm, along with the printing and advertising managers. His position was Lear-like. He had abandoned power but still attempted to exercise it. He was in an impossible dilemma. There had been a number of approaches to take over the paper by the large chain-newspaper firms. If the paper was left to members of the family who did not want to run it, it might well pass out of the family. On the other hand if it was to remain 'in the family' then some of the power had to pass out of the family into the hands of the professionals who had committed themselves to the paper in career terms and who had an interest in keeping the paper independent. But even this tended to accentuate the fact that, to put it figuratively, Reginald Wright was simply biding his time until he joined the melancholy throng on the back page.

Debrett had been a member of sporting and social clubs and had lived in the area when he had been in charge of the *Blacknoll* office as a young reporter. But when Wright brought him to work as deputy editor at the main office, he moved into the country and eventually became the secretary of the same conservation society as Reginald Wright. At Reginald's insistence, on becoming editor Debrett had stopped the reporters calling him by his first name and made them refer to him as Mr Debrett. The interesting thing about Debrett's career was its ambiguity and shades of regret. He had been offered jobs elsewhere on a number of occasions between returning from the services after the war and becoming editor. But he had always decided not to go. When asked why, he answered that he preferred life in a country town to a metropolitan rat-race. He stressed the fact that he knew his readers and they felt that the *Independent* was their paper. At the same time he could spend more time at home with his family, which he and his wife and children seemed to appreciate greatly. On other occasions, and especially after a particular dispute with Reginald Wright, his expressed attitude was almost diametrically opposed to this view. He had only ever stayed because of certain circumstances at the time: either on account of offers of higher wages and promotion by Reginald or for domestic reasons. He said he often felt he was 'getting out of touch' with what was happening in the world of journalism (he had ceased to be an officer in the National Union of Journalists on becoming editor). 'The only way you can keep in touch with what's going on is to maintain contact with old colleagues,' he would say wistfully. A number of his old workmates had become senior journalists on national dailies and regional evenings.

Sometimes, then, the rat-race was an attractive competitive event. And sometimes the situation at Littletown was stressful: Reginald Wright at one point, for instance, insisted on his final right to decide who should and who should not enter the building. Similarly, a scheme to introduce offset put forward by Debrett and Southall had been shelved indefinitely. Debrett was poised between two differing ideological commitments: on the one side his regret for missing out on the professional journalistic life with its mobility, its presence at the centre of events; and on the other, his home-centred, local commitment to Littletown and the *Independent*. The crucial advantage of Littletown was that he not only had a job, but the virtual certainty of eventually assuming control of the paper, which would give him an opportunity he would be unlikely to gain elsewhere.

Southall had had a similar career pattern in the sense that he had been on the point of moving on a number of occasions since coming to the *Independent* and likewise had been deterred either by the expense of buying a home in London or because he did not wish to change the children's schools. On the other hand he had moved around locally – he had worked for another paper nearby and for a time had worked outside journalism. He was now 'junior management' with a position on the board, but remained an active union member, notwithstanding his pessimism about being able to enforce union rules with Reginald Wright. Branch meetings of the union were a 'talking shop' enabling him to meet colleagues from other papers in the area including the nearest large newspaper, the *Evening Trumpet*. After the union meeting Southall and the three *Independent* reporters went for a drink together. They also dropped into the local pub regularly after putting the paper to bed on Friday and at lunchtime on Saturday.

Southall's connection with the 'management structure' was somewhat tenuous since at board meetings Reginald Wright more or less called the tune. Every Boxing Day, Southall and his family paid a traditional visit to Debrett at home, a continuation of the friendship since they had been young reporters together. Apart from this contact, Debrett's only outside work contacts with the staff were the usual office celebrations – birthdays, marriages, christenings, New Year's Eves, leaving parties.

There was then a diminishing amount of separation between the reporters and the *Independent* managerial establishment in descending order from Reginald, who kept aloof in work and in his social life; to Debrett, who was drawn into isolation partly by the demands which Reginald made in enforced formalism and exclusion in family life, and partly by the fact that he was 'home centred' and not a drinker. On the other hand in his working relationships, despite the fact that everyone except Southall called him Mr Debrett, he remained approachable and engaged in ribaldry and jocular interchanges, often making satiric references to 'old Reginald'. Then there was Southall, whose lot in most respects could be identified with that of his other working colleagues.

There were three full-time reporters at the Littletown office. One, Maurice Webb, had worked there for six years, and although he too had once considered moving he had retracted at the last moment and was now married and settled. Another Dave Young, still a junior with three years' service, planned to leave as soon as he had acquired his journalist's proficiency certificate and try initially for a job on an evening and eventually in Fleet Street as a sports writer. He had a thorough contempt for local affairs generally and especially for Reginald. The third, Bill Bennett, was a newly appointed junior fresh from school. The two district reporters both left and were replaced after short stays and did not impinge directly on life at Littletown.

All the reporters, including Southall, expressed an 'instrumental' attitude to the local organizations in that all of them were members of various local committees, but only in as much as this gave them access to stories and the committees access to publicity. They had been asked to be members by the committees. However, as soon as the meetings were over they left for home or the pub. It was the same at council meetings. If they were involved in the 'fabric of the community' it was very much in the pursuance of making a living in a congenial way with congenial colleagues, and not because they were committed to any of the Littletown causes. The only member of the staff so inclined had been Debrett, who had joined local social and charitable organizations in Blacknoll, but these activities had been curtailed because of Reginald's view of the incompatibility between local journalism and local involvement when Debrett took on editorial responsibility.

By examining a number of incidents in the paper's coverage of the town's life it is possible to throw into relief the negotiations, strategies, conflicts and accommodations which in the form of repeated interactional patterns made up the organizational life of the *Independent* office. Most stories come according to preordained patterns and the work proceeds invisibly. A reporter who has been to a council meeting the previous night typifies the events into stories, informs the editor and writes them up. Of the stories which reached the office from contacts nearly all came through Debrett, either because he was editor or was personally known to the local officials through his twenty-odd years as a journalist in the area. He simply passed on the story to a reporter, usually with instructions about whom to approach for more information and how to write it, in the sense that he would tell them how 'strong' it was to be – it might be needed at length for a page lead, or for a page one lead or perhaps only to fill a given space below the fold inside. The stories which did not follow these predetermined likes, however, make manifest the processes and power relations which underline the 'normal' story.

The bomb scare

One such story concerned a bomb scare. This involved a potential conflict between editor and contact and was resolved by a process of negotiation, in which the editor attempted to manoeuvre the contact into compliance. Although the *Independent* enjoyed monopoly coverage of Littletown, at Blacknoll their edition competed with a district edition of the neighbouring chain-newspaper weekly. In this competitive situation an 'exclusive' story is important, since journalists feel that the paper which consistently provides more news and advertisements relevant to the locality eventually triumphs. To those who have not taken part, a battle between two rival weekly newspapers in a small town may seem derisively comical: but it is a war of attribution, a zero sum game in which a number of reporters and other staff will succeed in gaining a high degree of job security while others will at least have to move within a company or perhaps be thrown out of work. In the 1960s especially the newspaper industry felt from the inside like a contracting world. The newspaper chain which ran the *Independent*'s competitor in Blacknoll had made take-over offers for the Wright business, so the frontier skirmishes in Blacknoll were potentially significant.

May Sharpe, poised in Blacknoll, phoned Debrett to tell him she had an exclusive story on a bomb hoax at the Plutex Chemical works (this was before the present IRA campaign in Britain). Plutex was a fertilizer plant with a highly explosive potential. She did not tell Debrett her source; nor did he ask, considering her an experienced reporter. When she tried to get a statement from the works manager he refused to say anything. His factory was part of a bigger group and any statement would have to come from the press relations officer at headquarters. What should she do, she wanted to know. Debrett said he would deal with the matter. He did not want a press statement issued by the Plutex headquarters since that would kill the story's exclusiveness and result in television, radio and the evening papers having the story out before the *Independent* even went to press.

He rang up the manager, introduced himself as the editor and asked for a statement and details of what had happened. The manager said: 'We are both responsible men in responsible positions and we realize the sort of unfortunate results that can come from publicity about this kind of thing. You know, imitation and so on.' He asked Debrett to think about it and ring him back. Debrett agreed to wait and consider the matter, although he never had any intention of not publishing. He could get the details about the time and place of the malicious false alarm, as well as of the numbers of people evacuated from the factory, from the police and the fire-brigade. But he needed information from the manager about the nature of the plant and a statement for quoting to make the story satisfy journalistic norms. Such a statement would also constitute a form of consent: there would be no come-back from the company afterwards in terms of complaints or failure to co-operate on other stories.

He waited for an hour, which he regarded as a respectable time for cogitation, and then rang back. He said that after thinking about it he had decided to go ahead with the story. He explained that the story would be 'responsible' and would show that the hoaxer had caused a lot of inconvenience to everyone including himself. It would stress that the whole incident was not worth the trouble of getting caught. To underline his public-spirited approach he emphasized that members of the public who had seen anything suspicious might respond to the story by coming forward with information. Of course if he had been genuinely concerned primarily with public safety he should have been quite happy for Plutex to issue a public statement to the other media, since that would have made public response far more probable. The manager agreed, and gave Debrett the details of how the hoax was perpetrated, of the workers involved and the time lost. He added a condemnation of the malicious caller. The story appeared across five columns at the top of the front page of the *Independent* under the headline 'SOMEONE WITH A VERY SICK MIND'.

This incident draws attention to a number of points concerning the organization and power relationship of such a paper. First the reporter's role does not include representing the paper in negotiations with a high-status individual over a story. The editor's competence extends into this field and underlines his position as a 'gatekeeper' in relation to other contacts. That is, he is normally interposed between contacts and reporters and this increases his power over reporters in the office. The reporter may make the original contact and get the story, but anything hinting of trouble brings in the editor as arbiter. Here the negotiation took place because the obtaining of the story was of a non-routine nature. It did not fit into the usual predictable process of following up a lead with an interview, with a co-operative approach. Debrett took over in part because of this non-routine element and his manoeuvres involved an attempt to structure the interaction with the manager around some appropriate rules both for the process and the outcome of negotiations. In negotiating with the manager Debrett played the status game. In announcing himself as the editor he was saying 'I am worth talking to' and warning that certain types of stratagem would not be appropriate as put-offs. The manager on the other hand responded with a status stratagem – 'We are both responsible men'. Thus the negotiations took place as a series of manoeuvres around the significance of the concepts of responsibility, with its components of power and altruism. This story illustrates both how the allocation of tasks at the *Independent* was related to the distribution and how these factors were reflected in interaction with contacts.

The troublesome quarries

Over the years the *Independent*, originally through its leader, which had gone by the board since Reginald Wright's retirement, and subsequently through the former editor's column, had waged a campaign against the extension of the quarrying which was a feature of the landscape around Blacknoll. Wright and Debrett were of course also interested in the issue as conservationists. As a matter of form every time a quarrying firm put in a planning application to extend its activities it was turned down by local planning authority. If they wished to challenge the decision the companies had to appeal to the then Minister of Housing and Local Government (now Secretary of State for the Environment). Then in the late 1960s for the first time the planning committee granted a request for an extension of a quarry. Local residents, hoping to oppose the move, claimed they were told by county council officials that they could not appeal against the granting of permission to a third party since they had no direct interest in the site. However, some of them, dissatisfied with such a state of affairs, consulted a solicitor and found they could appeal at any time until the actual confirmation of the decision by the Minister of Housing.

Debrett himself was covering the story partly because it was a continuation of the story he had first covered as a young reporter at Blacknoll and he therefore knew the background. Secondly the issue affected rural conservation in the area. His main interest, however, seemed to be as a journalist. He became aware of the story when looking through the council minutes and realized that planning permission was being granted to a quarry extension for the first time. He made inquiries with Blacknoll borough council officials and members of the anti-quarry lobby, both of whom he had known since he was a young reporter.

The anti-quarry lobby asked Debrett not to reveal that they were fighting the case, because they wanted the county council to have as little warning as possible. They feared that in the event of being given warning the council might try to rush through the decision with the ministry and pre-empt any opposition. They thought the county council officials believed that their story about not being able to appeal against the approval of a planning permission had been accepted. They had in other words developed a conspiracy ideology and were double-bluffing the county council officials who were cast in the role of co-conspirators with the quarry interests.

Debrett accepted their request, simply reporting briefly the formal approval of the planning application. And he did more. On his own account he contacted the area's Tory MP, Sir Arnold Rawlings, who got in touch with the minister and with the county council. He then wrote a story for the next issue on Rawlings's activities, without mentioning his own intervention. When the anti-quarry lobby's solicitors acted to institute a public inquiry to appeal against the decision Debrett again reported this. In holding back what he knew, he had earned the goodwill of the anti-quarry lobby who were a permanent source of news; if he had offended the county council this did not matter. Very little news in the *Independent* came from this source. Further, he had got additional mileage out of the story from the MP who had in turn been blessed with some favourable publicity.

Debrett in this case was able to take over completely tasks normally associated with a reporter – to wit, the writing of the story. He was also able to deal with Rawlings, an old friend of Reginald Wright who occupied the same right-wing political ground, without Reginald's intervention. Debrett himself had had a long association with Rawlings, although this was restricted to professional contacts.

In other words in the execution of the day-to-day editorial affairs of the paper Debrett was the final, although not the sole, arbiter of events. In this case he could participate in the creation of news, ignore county council officials, put off publishing material for a variety of motives: political, organizational, economic, ideological.

The defence of England: tilting at windmills

The *Independent* since its Victorian inception had been committed to a non-partisan support for all things Littletownian. In the pre-war period central government intervention to alleviate unemployment; after the war a campaign for Littletown's veterans; and a continual pressure for the encouragement of industrial employment in the area; help for its farmers. Littletown first, then England: Littletown as quintessential England: England as Littletown writ large. Then the United Kingdom: there was an Irishman (in the Iniskilling Fusiliers) a Scotsman (Royal Howards) and a Welshman (Welsh Guards), and they were good fellows all. Of course there were others: long-haired intellectuals and the like; types who wanted to prevent the Springboks' tour – 'the finest rugby players in the world' – or types who jibed at our kith and kin doing their bit for civilization in Rhodesia. These sort of undesirables were likely to cop it from Reginald's pen which he dipped each week into slightly *démodé* vitriol. Reginald was no true-blue caricature Tory; nor a fascist. He was not even a Gaullist. He was more a mini-de Gaulle; through the medium of the *Independent* he embodied the 'essential genius' of Littletown. His attitude to central government was a strange paradox; he might be lambasting them for doing too little, or intervening too much. His criteria for judgement appeared to be whether its activities would benefit Littletown, although his Littletown rarely seemed to be that of the Wimpey-type commuter estates around the town, nor of the welfare state, trade unionized factory workers on their new industrial estates.

One of his most consistent and strongly fought campaigns was against the closure of the local war memorial hospital. It carried on through the last years of his own editorship and survived like an institution into Debrett's. When a newspaper engages in a campaign, it involves two types of activity: (a) manifest pontification in support of its aims and (b) the raising to prominence of stories or features about the issue at stake. When a scheme for the closure of the hospital erected to the memory of the town's war heroes was first put forward in the early 1960s by the Conservative government, Reginald attacked the scheme in an editorial leader column. He also gave generous coverage to the activities of the town's hospital protection committee. Petition forms were printed on Wright's presses at the expense of the *Independent* and delivered along with the news-papers throughout Littletown. Petitions were then filled in and returned to the *Independent* office and passed on to the authorities. The plan was deferred, but governments of succeeding years, moving towards a national policy of large general hospitals catering for wider areas of the country than Littletown, apparently had the memorial hospital marked down for eventual disbandment. Then eight years after the first skirmish, and now under Debrett's editor-ship, there appeared the headline 'NOW IT'S WAR'. This Churchillian legend referred to a conflict between the Ministry of Health and the local council, as a result of an imminent proposal by the central authorities to go ahead with their reorganization. A fortnight later there appeared a page-one story under the somewhat fanciful headline 'NOW THE DEAD FIGHT FOR HOSPITAL'. This recounted how the local defenders of the hospital were marshalling troops from beyond the grave by pressing into service the roll-call of Littletown's slaughtered warriors.

A fortnight later, Reginald, having kept his powder dry and now seeing the whites of the enemy's eyes, opened fire in his personal column. The government was blamed for wanting to destroy Littletown's link with its martial past. Two weeks later the military leitmotiv reappeared in the fanfare 'LET BATTLE COMMENCE' over a front-page story on the setting up of another hospital defence committee. A week later Reginald up-ended his cannon and fired into the air with a barrel of canister-shot which exploded over the heads of his new allies and sprayed them with what threatened to be stinging buckshot but fell out as confetti. Commenting on the committee he observed: '. . . its constitution so far irresistibly reminds us of what the Duke of Wellington said when reviewing some of the scratch troops prior to the battle of Waterloo. "I don't know what the enemy will think of them," he said, "but by God they frighten me." We sincerely hope this impression will prove to be completely unjustified but the enemy in this case is certainly not one who is easily frightened.'

However, the comment might more aptly have applied to the writer of the piece and the paper, rather than the committee. For in the same issue there was a story which appeared to mean either that the local committee had been victorious or the whole affair had been a mare's-nest. There, stripped of all military metaphor, stood a story, 'LOCAL HOSPITAL NOT IN JEOPARDY – MINISTER', which paraphrased an extract from *Hansard* sent to Debrett by Sir Arnold Rawlings that recounted a junior minister's reply to that MP's question on the subject of the hospital. The reply stated that the hospital was not in danger of closure but had only a 65 per cent occupancy. The failure to fill the hospital, said the minister, was the responsibility of the local hospital management board. The reason for the fact that Reginald Wright was still fighting a battle while everyone else had left the field was that he did not actually take part in writing the paper and had to read each issue before commenting in it. His articles were thus always a week out of date. During the campaign, the hospital defence committee's only contact with the paper was the delivery of handouts saying what happened at the meeting and the original announcement that the committee had been formed. The *Independent* was in a passive role so far as the news-getting process was concerned: the importance of the story appeared to be related to the paper's tradition set down in the 1890s and carried on without a break by Reginald (who was also of the 1890s vintage), that any local interest should be pushed with immoderate enthusiasm. More specifically Debrett was carrying out a campaign which had been started by Reginald. The campaign was a conditioned reflex; the issue of the hospital and a local defence committee reproduced the battle-cries of eight years before. No one actually checked, for instance, how many beds were occupied, what cases were dealt with, or what the ministry's plans were. The committee's handouts and Rawlings's letter were their sole univerified sources.

Shortly after the memorial hospital campaign ended, with speeches by the Iron Duke and an under-secretary of state at the Ministry of Health, another campaign got under way. A letter appeared in the correspondence column of the *Independent* from an architectural student, Gerald Henig. It claimed that the council was about to demolish Tudor Folly, a building of architectural and historic interest, which was also capable of renovation, in order to widen a road. A week later, after he had read the paper, Reginald Wright took up the cudgels in his column. He supported Henig's claim and called for the renovation of the Tudor building. A week later Debrett ran on the front page a two-column caption story under an artist's impression by Henig, showing Tudor Folly as it was under a skin of pealing stucco – a fine example of a ribbed, timber-frame house. That night, the appropriate council committee met and considered two schemes for saving the building, which according to the borough surveyor, was (a) in the way of a necessary road-widening scheme (b) derelict and (c) already partly demolished.

The first renovation scheme by Henig was costed at £7,000; and the second by an architect, Mr F. Greenwood, and an associate, Mr R. B. Wright, was costed at £12,000. The committee decided to go ahead with the demolition without consulting the interested parties. The story appeared in the next issue of the *Independent* under the headline 'BID TO SAVE TUDOR COTTAGE FAILS'. The story quoted a letter to the council from R. B. Wright (without identifying him as Reginald Wright, proprietor of the newspaper) and this was

T.S.W.—D

in the context of an article which balanced almost exactly the pro and anti statements, in terms of numbers of column inches. But the tone of the article gave the strong impression of attributing reason and cogency to the council's plan.

Southall, who wrote the article, used his powers of paraphrase to draw together the council's case, whereas the conservationist case had to rely on Reginald's letter. The council also had figures and arguments which came out of a consideration of the letters and schemes; they had the answers, the last word. Southall did not go to either Henig or Wright for a comment on the committee decision: 'When it was suggested . . . that to have the derelict house restored would cost as much as £12,000, members voted in favour of demolition,' his story ran. Here the juxtaposition of the words 'derelict' and 'as much as' with the decision to demolish are a sort of buried comment implying rationality on the part of the council. Substitute 'historic' for 'derelict' and 'as little as' for 'as much as' and you have a totally different bias.

The report continued: 'Demolition had already begun on the house – which stands in the way of a road improvement scheme at the bottom of Daveney Road – when efforts started to save it. They (the committee) seemed to feel, however, that restoration would result in only a pseudo-Tudor building remaining and it was felt in some quarters that the work would involve an almost complete rebuilding programme on the existing timbers which would have to be strengthened with steel girders.'

The committee's case was thus put forward without its being attributed to any one member – what was 'felt in some quarters' is a journalist's ploy for saying what the reporter himself feels or for converting into 'good English' a case which might be embarrassingly incoherent if reported verbatim. Finally it is a technique for reporting the views of a council official who is supposed to be disinterested. In this case Southall was doing all three. He had spoken to the council surveyor who thought the campaign to save the building was ridiculous. So did Southall. But he 'improved' what was said at the meeting in order to draw together into a neater argument an encapsulated version of the surveyor's and his own opinions.

There was a good deal to recommend Southall's position. The house had been found unsuitable for listing as an historic building by the Ministry of Works in 1950, because even then it was already very delapidated. However, two houses immediately adjoining it were listed as historic buildings. The owner of Tudor Folly had at that time been told by the council that he should put his house in good repair, purely as a public safeguard. Two years prior to the campaign the council bought the house to make way for the road widening. The surveyor's report showed that only the frame was capable of salvation; and this was infested by woodworm and would be unsafe without support by RSJS. The conservationists' only suggestion for the house was to convert it into a museum, but no detailed scheme was put forward; the council's road-widening scheme was written off as hardly 'necessary'. By the time Reginald discovered the issue of Tudor Folly it had been under a specific demolition order for two years and a potential issue for nearly twenty years (since the original Ministry of Works decision in 1950). By the time he turned his pen to the issue all that remained of the building was a part-demolished ruin, presented by Reginald as a piece of Merrie England subject to imminent depredation by local government vandals. The only support from the local population as a result of the campaign was an anonymous *offer* of £25 which Reginald referred to in his letter to the council committee, an offer which was the nearest thing to material aid to meet a cost put at a minimum of £4,000 by the amenitarians and at £12,000 by the council.

Unlike the case of the memorial hospital the journalists were not simply carrying out a ritualized form of behaviour vis-à-vis a specific issue. They were not even applying some general behavioural typification of events and 'conducting a campaign'. Debrett was disinterested; he supposed there were two sides to the argument. Left to himself, he did not bother to make a story of the original letter. On the other hand, a fortnight later after he had read Reginald Wright's column he did so with an artist's impression of the house, which Henig brought in, having been encouraged by Reginald's column. Strangely, there was no behind-the-scenes collusion: the progression of stimulus and response among all three was done at weekly intervals through reading the newspapers. Debrett was a gatekeeper in the sense that he dealt with Henig's letters and accepted the picture from him. But his response to Henig after Reginald's proselytizing was conditioned by his knowledge that he was a person who espoused a cause dear to the proprietor's heart. Southall, on the other hand, although not susceptible to a Reginaldized version of reality, nonetheless was sucked into Reginald's scheme of priorities: since he had to write up a story at length confounding the conservationist case which had only been made prominent owing to Reginald's direct or indirect influence. Under normal circumstances the story would only have run to a paragraph or two.

After the council's decision to go ahead two letters appeared in the letters-to-the-editor column from Henig and Greenwood. Apart from them and Reginald only the anonymous offerer of £25 had given any evidence of being concerned about the fate of Tudor Folly. In almost every sense it was a story and an issue created by the *Independent*.

The 'no visitors' rule

On the issue of private property Reginald's devotion to propriety approached the fanatical. He demanded strict control over who came into the building. No one was to be allowed into the paper's file-room to look up old copies without being accompanied by a member of staff. No outsider was allowed to be in the reporters' room: interviews were to be carried out in the 'interview-room', a cubby-hole off the main shop front. At the same time, in theory Debrett was supposed to have editorial control of the paper, untrammelled by any interference from Reginald Wright.

In the matter of the 'no visitors' rule, Debrett was drawn into the ambit of Southall and the other reporters, and this can be exemplified by one of the ways in which the rule actually affected the editorial organization of the paper. The reporters at the *Independent* ran a 'linage pool': they sold stories to nationals and evenings on a regular basis. Debrett knew about this and both encouraged and controlled it. He encouraged it for the – editorially speaking – good reason that it encouraged his staff to seek out good stories, to learn how to dress up otherwise drab stories as good stories, and it 'kept them on the ball'. On the other hand he controlled it because (a) he did want the efforts of his reporters directed in a major part of the week to writing material for other papers and (b) he did not want them 'to kill their own goose' – to put stories into the dailies which were published before the *Independent*. Tip-offs and copy of original stories (those non-routine or human interest stories coming out of the *Independent*'s knowledge of the area) were therefore sent out after the paper went to bed but before it was in the newsagents. The practice of 'licensing' linage appears to be virtually universal in the British local weekly press.

One regular visitor to the office on this account was Jock Laing, a representative of a national daily who used to call on Thursdays to see if there was anything which might interest him. If a story were brewing and Debrett wanted it for the following week he would negotiate with Laing about the time they would give him the details. Debrett, who had of course done linage as a young reporter, was directly involved in the dealings with Laing and would go into the reporters' room with others when Laing came. If there were no business to discuss they might sit and chat amiably. One week, apparently, Reginald Wright came down unexpectedly to the reporters' room and saw Laing. The others, seeing him fix the outsider with a gimlet stare of inquiry, volunteered that he was a typewriter salesman, and all including Laing and Debrett carried off the charade.

Reginald's demand that visitors to the file-room must be accompanied by a member of staff also conflicted with Debrett's very open policy which sprang both from a desire to maintain good public relations and from a genuine interest in local history and scholarship. If any students or teachers found the file-room a useful source of data for projects, essays or theses Debrett would go out of his way to be helpful. He regarded the newspaper as being part of the local establishment in the sense that it formed a link between the people, the council and the courts. Moreover, he regarded the office itself as being capable of providing a public service. He would even go to some personal lengths to provide inquirers with information, sometimes as a result of inquiries through his journalistic contacts built up over the years. This direct conflict of attitudes towards the privacy of the office eventually led to a row in which Debrett gave back the key to the file-room and insisted that the old man guarded his own property.

In this area (the rules about visitors) Debrett was drawn into an alliance with the reporters, while his management position drew him into a sort of crippled loyalty to Reginald. His actual relationship with Reginald was equally ambiguous. Over executive decisions, whether or not to 'go offset', Reginald appeared to be the final arbiter. In matters of editorial policy Debrett appeared to have a control over events springing from his professional day-to-day activities, while Reginald exerted an evermore attenuated pull through the influence of his column and by reason of tradition. Reginald's power was seen as final by the reporters, because he was the proprietor. But the very isolation he used to underline his socially elevated position meant that he was excluded from the communications network of his junior staff. This in turn meant that they could thwart his power to enforce rules: while he, through ignorance, was impotent to control their work practices. Only Debrett could do this because of his access to their communications network.

The division of ownership and control was more than a mere trick of light. Reginald could not censor everything that went into the paper without finding something to replace it – that is, without re-establishing himself as editor. What action if any he would have taken had Debrett done something radical to the editorial style of the paper was purely a matter for speculation, and in any event Debrett's assessment of the market for and the role of the paper made any counter-measures highly improbable.

It is possible to regard the *Littletown Independent* as a relatively simple news-processing organization. Diagram 1 is intended to clarify the relationship so far depicted. When the parties are included within boundaries, this indicates that co-operative interaction within the boundary was a normal feature of organizational or power

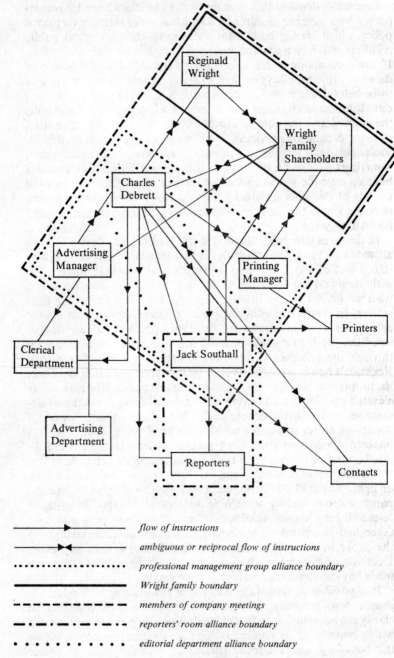

flow of instructions

ambiguous or reciprocal flow of instructions

professional management group alliance boundary

Wright family boundary

members of company meetings

reporters' room alliance boundary

editorial department alliance boundary

DIAGRAM 1

LITTLETOWN INDEPENDENT: ORGANIZATIONAL INTERACTION

relationships. When the boundaries are broken this indicates that there were also overt manifestations of distance or antagonism. Southall's position, for instance, is clarified by this representation. He interacts in a normally co-operative way with Debrett as part of the managerial structure and both socially and occupationally with the reporters who were in many situations antagonistic to Reginald Wright, who was for them the embodiment of management.

In terms of the flow of instructions Debrett is seen as being at a nodal position both in terms of direct and indirect contacts. Reginald Wright's connection into the organizational set-up was primarily through Debrett, and this was ambiguous in terms of power. On the other hand his connection with the Wright family, with whom he owned the bulk of the company, gave him an independent source of power in terms of sheer ownership. But this mainly gave him power to dispose of the business which was something he did not wish to do. Both Debrett and Southall were in nodal positions in the organization: the difference between them is in terms of their formal power (which as we shall see in the next chapter may often not be directly related to behaviour) and the use they made of the nodality – Debrett for controls, Southall as a social resource.

In formulating an analysis of comparison between the *Independent* and the *Blackville Examiner,* two analytical categories have been employed: role and process. These provide sufficiently general categories to cope with (a) the differences in business form and (b) the specificity of the data under consideration. They also provide a means of relating the aims, values and modes of structuring reality of individuals with the economic activities they engage in.

In looking at role-playing we shall examine the orientations of actors to situations of interaction and the type of interaction. In looking at processes we shall consider how the tasks involved in producing stories and papers are divided between actors, and the extent to which any given actor interposes himself at crucial points in the chain of tasks making up the process. Both roles and processes are seen as being made up of tasks: in the case of the role they are orientated to the actor; in the case of the process they are related in the outcome. In normal circumstances the process of producing and publishing a news story at the *Independent* would involve the reporter in interaction with a contact; structuring the data into an account in accordance with the norms of a 'good story' and passing it on to the editor or deputy editor who would sub-edit it and place it in the paper. However, there are a number of other events we have seen which can occur in the process. It may be necessary to engage in bargaining or negotiation, as in the bomb-scare story; or checking with contacts, as in the case of the troublesome quarries. The editor, as we have seen may intervene at almost any point which strikes him while he is actually subbing a story and check it with a contact. Finally a story may produce a further contact and possibly a follow-up.

Interaction between a journalist and contact takes a number of different forms. Sometimes it may be entirely a written affair perhaps hardly worth describing as interaction: the reporter receives a written piece of information from a contact which he processes into a story, both by structuring it into a 'good story' and by compliance with the particular demands of space and time laid down by the editor (e.g. 'Write this up as a two-par piece, I've got a little space on the front page to fill.'). The contact then reads the story and if it is acceptable either does nothing or waits until he has something else to report, when he does the same thing again. The reporter is in a similar role when he is simply a listener, as in court or council meetings. In one-off cases the reporter probably receives a tip-off from a reader or a regular contact such as the police or fire-brigade and then he has to interview victims, eye-witnesses and others who are involved. In both 'listening' interaction and the reception of written statements the stories may often arise out of long-term professional relationships between newspapermen and their sources. One-offs involving tips from the police or fire-brigade are the result of long-cultivated interaction, often involving specific rituals and long-standing personal knowledge.

We have looked at cases involving relatively overt interaction, since these do tend to make explicit what is normally reflexible and tacit. Where this occurs we can break down the interaction between journalist and client into a number of elements:

(a) Contact
(b) Identification
(c) Bargaining
(d) Collection of data

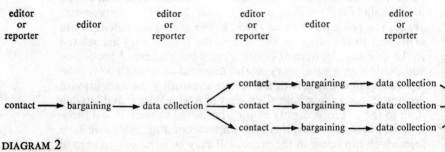

DIAGRAM 2
LITTLETOWN INDEPENDENT: TASK ALLOCATION IN PUBLICATION OF NEWS ITEMS

These elements may co-occur as strands in conversation – or they may become so clearly distinct as to be identified as different tasks to be undertaken by different actors. They may be clarified more fully.

(a) *Contact*: this refers simply to the initial stage where the reporter locates the news source or the news source locates the journalist.

(b) *Identification*: this refers both to the contact or the journalist identifying themselves and identifying the other. The reason for identification is basically to state one's own purpose and use and to find out the purpose and use of the other actor. It may rely on certain common assumptions, although it is not to be regarded as part of a rule-making or rule-identifying process. Identification is a signal as to whether or not other procedures should be undertaken. For instance the statement 'this is the editor speaking' can mean 'you can complain to me', 'you can discuss things with me', 'I can tell you what we're going to do here', or 'if you want future coverage, I'm the man with power to give it or refuse it'.

(c) *Bargaining*: this concerns the competitive/co-operative process by which journalists attempt to get information from contacts and by which the contact gets favourable publicity out of the journalist or attempts to prevent him from publishing something the contact does not like.

(d) *Collection of data*: this is not an unambiguous process. It may well be mixed up with identification and bargaining. The data which are collected are related to both the preconceptions which the journalist brings to story and the 'technical' economic demands of his job as he perceives them.

reporter   editor
or   or
editor   deputy

```
formulation                                                                                    receive
data ──→ sub-editing ──→ re-contact ──→ bargaining ──→ rewrite ──→ layout ──→ publish ──→  complaint
story
```

Let us now consider the context of this interaction as part of the news-manufacturing process involving all the possibilities (such as follow-up contacts) which we have considered so far (see Diagram 2, p. 104). What is apparent from Diagram 2 is that the editor at the *Independent* has tasks which are exclusively his, but the reporter, although he has tasks which are legitimately his own, does not have exclusive control over them. For instance, Debrett could simply decide to cover the quarries story from beginning to end and the reporter could not protect even his own beat from such an encroachment. Second, once a story passes the sub-editing stage it goes into an area which (apart from the purely technical tasks of reading and checking 'on the stone',* done by the reporters at Littletown) is exclusively in the province of the editor. In this respect the only writer who had exclusive control over his material up to this point was Reginald Wright. Afterwards even his material had at times been cut for reasons of space. Third, it is apparent that to regard the paper as a bounded system is unrealistic. Contacts are potentially active participants in the production process at a number of points. Of course in the run-of-the-mill story they only come into it at one point. In a sense the most clean-cut boundary is that excluding the reporter from certain tasks. This is not to deny that reporters in other contexts carry on excluding practices related to the production of stories, an aspect which will be discussed later. Fourth, in the pre-sub-editing stages those areas of competence which the editor arrogates exclusively to himself are those involving negotiations with contacts where a non-routine decision is required. This interaction involves a status game which underlines Debrett's identity as an actor with whom a contact is going to get in touch after publication and, at the same time, as the man to whom reporters take difficult cases.

In short, the organization of news gathering at the *Littletown Independent* was formally simple, but in terms of interaction, complex. There was a downward flowing ambiguity about the tasks and power attaching to roles. Reporters could exercise no exclusive control over either their tasks or their autonomy because the editor could extend his activity into their normal areas of competence. Inasmuch as he suffered ambiguity in the enactment of the editorial role this was because of his interaction with the proprietor whose presence involved limits on managerial control. This situation was in turn reflected in the division of the production process. The points at which the flow of production passed from one specialism to another were ambiguous, but while the greatest ambiguity existed about the early 'raw material' part of the process, the least attached to high-status presentation tasks at the final stages.

*The 'stone' is the bench on which the compositor sets the pages in metal.

6
The *Blackville Examiner*

If you see a photograph of a grimy industrial town on the cover of a socially committed novel, an economic history book or a sociological study of strikes, deprivation or bad housing, it will probably be Blackville. In general design and structure it typifies all the industrial ills of Britain which became cinematic clichés in certain documentary films of the 1950s. Of recent years its pristine dinginess and picturesque slums have fallen victim to civic pride and domestic hygiene. But it still remains a starkly grim and gloomy contrast to a semirural backwater such as Littletown.

Organization and technology

The town's newspaper, the *Blackville Examiner*, with a circulation of over 40,000 was one of the biggest local weeklies in the country. Latterly it was owned by Macro-Type Ltd, which took it over from the Blagg family who had run it as a family concern until the mid-1960s. The instant and remarkable difference between the *Examiner* and the *Independent* was in their physical setting. In place of the quaint office in the small town high street which housed the *Independent*, was a modern windswept factory with offices in a new industrial estate surrounded by galloping dereliction, in the form of the brick-ends and broken glass of the Industrial Revolution. The main part of the building contained a modern offset printing plant with expensive colour equipment, while the reporters, administrators and advertising departments were housed in a small block of offices at one end of the site. The reporters had their own room, which was about six times as large in floor area as that at the *Independent*. The two sub-editors and deputy editor had another office: the editor occupied an office between the reporters' room and the subs' room. They also had a library where the files of old papers were kept (not very systematically) and an interview-room.

This generous space was in part needed because of the size of the editorial department, which was twice as big as that of the *Independent*, but was more a reflection of the departmental specialization which existed at Blackville to a degree quite remarkable for a local weekly paper. There were six reporters based in the reporters' room, and among these the chief reporter, Tony Radcliffe, was formally in charge. His main responsibility was to see that each job was covered, and this meant drawing a list at the beginning of each week of work to be done with the initials of a reporter attached to each event. This was the result of asking reporters what their jobs were going to be rather than assigning them work. Once the reporters had covered their jobs and written their material their work was done; the subs were then responsible for checking, deciding on typeface and headlines for stories assigned to them and for laying out their own pages. Mike Williams, the deputy editor, co-ordinated their work, laid out his own pages and liaised with Radcliffe. In theory the editor, Charlie Plowden, had overall control, wrote the leaders, a column of diary comment and feature and laid it out in the leader page.

This bureaucratized system of management worked to a set of deadlines. Each person in the editorial department had an indentified set of tasks which had to be completed by a given time. This meant that in the event of a failure of the paper to meet such a deadline the person responsible was identifiable. This may sound a draconian system but in effect, as we shall see, was quite the reverse. One of the reasons for the system was that Macro-Type also printed the *Hillburgh Globe* on the *Examiner*'s presses. Each compositor had his working week allocated by days or half-days to pages of the *Globe* or the *Examiner*. By this full use of the plant Macro hoped the quicker to recoup the cost of taking over the *Examiner*. Equally, by operating strictly to deadlines and thus avoiding working overtime they kept down labour costs.

Such a system did of course put a high premium on predictability of editorial content. News, being less predictable than feature articles, is not suitable material if you need a steady flow throughout the week. Consequently there was a regular diet of features, news features and background news to feed the presses. A reporter writing a feature on the social history of allotments in Blackville, or a descriptive piece on a police night-shift, can guarantee in advance with the addition of pictures to fill a page or part of one by a given time, in a way that would not be possible in covering a council meeting which might contain nothing newsworthy or a fire which might not happen.

This mode of operation had consequences for role-playing and interaction by the editorial staff which differentiated it markedly from the *Littletown Independent*. The set-up at Blackville was inherited by Macro from the Blagg family. The general manager, Harry Ransom, negotiated the take-over of the staff and the working system so that he could retain managerial control, Charlie Plowden the editorship, and the other managerial staff their own respective spheres of control. The only new human element in the managerial situation was the accountant Philip Snow who had been appointed by the corporation after the take-over.

Prior to the take-over Ransom, who had married into the Blagg family, only had to deal with family board meetings. In a real sense he was a victim of his own success. The paper accumulated sufficient capital over a period of seven years to buy outright the new factory and offices along with all the new printing and type-setting plant, apart from the colour printing machinery, which had to be paid for on a loan. At the same time the company retained the ownership of the original office in the town centre. This occurred before the boom in property values at the end of the 1960s. Had Blaggs remained independent they would doubtless have reaped a considerable harvest and indeed as a business venture the paper continued to prosper after the take-over with increased sales and advertising revenue. The company was attractive to Macro-Type who already owned another paper in Blackville. At the same time the offers made by Macro-Type to the Blagg family became more attractive, especially as several of them had need of some of the immediate large cash sums being offered. The majority of the family succumbed, and Ransom and his wife were dragged protestingly into the corporate society.

Now Ransom, instead of dealing with the family at their meetings, faced corporate control in the shape of the Macro-Type bureaucracy in London. This took two forms: directional interference in specific decisions; specific rules of behaviour limiting Ransom's power in his managerial role. The most obvious directional interference took the form of staffing allocations and directing changes in work schedules. When a new national agreement was arrived at between the printing unions and employers, Macro-Type instructed the *Blackville Examiner* to bring forward its deadlines and if a deadline was missed by half an hour a complaint was sent from central office to Blackville. The fact of printing two papers at Blackville added a visibly critical quality to these deadlines, and the tight system of production control made identification from a distance relatively straightforward.

On other occasions such direct interaction was more difficult. Macro-Type owned another office and printing works in Blackville where they published an edition of a regional evening paper, the *Northern Evening Gazette*. The corporation planners decided that a more efficient deployment of manpower in Blackville could be attained by using the same reporters to cover court cases, council meetings and other diary jobs for both papers. The result would have been almost certainly fewer journalistic jobs, and a reduction in managerial power at the *Examiner*. Fearing these consequences, Ransom, with the support of all the management at the *Examiner* office, told Macro-Type that such an alteration in working practice was impossible because the *Examiner* required different coverage from the *Evening Gazette*, and that the weekly paper was only able to survive as a profitable busines by its identity as an independent, visibly different newspaper from the *Gazette*: if this distinction disappeared it might well cease to be profitable, he argued. In this argument Ransom was successful, despite the fact that the reporters already operated such a labour-saving system, but one which they controlled without management's knowledge or intervention, as will be shown later.

The rules of managerial conduct required Ransom to fit Macro's bureaucratic mould: to provide information to head office and to refrain from unsanctioned policy innovation. He had to send circulation figures, financial returns compiled by the accountant, Philip Snow, half-yearly capital equipment requisitions, advertising figures and staffing returns. However, in practice this often meant constructing reality in accordance with these organizational demands rather than actually altering his policy. For instance, a proposed extension which was required was applied for by Ransom at an inflated cost of £15,000, and this was cut back to £10,000. Such a figure was acceptable in the first place, but it was necessary to ask for a more prodigal scheme in order to get the sum originally required and at the same time appear to accept Macro's control. Another capital expansion which would have cost more than the financial limit on unsanctioned expenditure was obtained by putting it through in several stages below this limit. Plowden, the editor, Mike Williams his deputy, Bonsor the works manager, and Clegg the advertising manager had all worked in their present capacities with Ransom at Blaggs. Clearly Snow was an 'outsider' and his position was influential. He had to prepare all the accounts for submission to Macro, and his responsibility for any failure in this direction would of course be direct to Macro and not to Ransom. He also had charge of the administration at Blackville. This part of the office along with advertising staff had increased more than threefold since the take-over and administrators and advertisers outnumbered the editorial department by nearly three to one.

Editorially, Plowden's actual power as distinct from his formal position appeared to be almost nominal. He had been ill and was due to retire shortly. The change from a traditional family newspaper to a large chain operation with new printing methods appeared to have come at the wrong time for him to adjust, and he left the day-to-day running of the paper to Mike Williams. Reporters asking him for information or instructions were continually referred to Williams as the appropriate decision-maker. Plowden's decline in activity was accompanied by the continued prosperity of the paper and its efficient operation by Mike Williams, who readily undertook the work. In the context of the *Examiner* he was ambitious. He had committed his working life to the paper and everyone expected that he would step into Plowden's shoes when the old man retired. During the previous five or ten years, without any formal change in status he had taken on the tasks previously associated with the editorial role in the traditional newspaper set-up, and the new tasks appropriate to the role which derived from the technological and organizational change through which the paper was going. The traditional tasks were those of taking charge of layout, supervision of sub-editing and of the reporters' work through his link with Radcliffe. The new organization and technology meant that he had to be responsible for marrying printing and editorial work schedules, and for the co-ordination of the two editorial sub-departments' reporters and sub-editors to meet the page deadlines.

When Williams was away on holiday his work was taken over primarily by the longer serving sub-editor, Bill Bradley, although some extra work was done by Plowden. Bradley was an active union member and his relationships with the reporters were on an apparently equalitarian basis, although the reporters suspected him of secret ambition. At twenty-six, Alf Peters was the most junior sub-editor. He went drinking in the evenings with Tony Radcliffe, with whom he had previously also been a fellow-mountaineer. Radcliffe was already married and Peters gave rise to general office amusement when in order to raise the money for his own wedding, he spent his holidays selling newspapers. In general he was a gossip and a man of levity who entertained no visible ambitions and professed himself satisfied with his lot.

The six reporters, including Radcliffe, were all NUJ members, as were Williams and the subs. Plowden was an associate member. Radcliffe's chief reportership involved him only in fixing names to jobs in the schedule so that they could be checked off as they were done and inquiries about progress made to the appropriate reporter. He never gave orders and appeared most concerned to lead a quiet life. His place when away was taken by Bertram Guest who had no officially differentiated status and was in fact the second youngest member of the reporting staff. Fred Maxwell, one of the four remaining reporters, was in his mid-forties and an encyclopedic authority on Blackville; he was also a highly entertaining raconteur with a repository of ribald jokes, and had had a varied background including face-work in the mines. Left-wing politically, he was short, hairy and strongly built, worked with his short-sleeves rolled up over simian arms, and spoke with one hand on his bared braces and a Woodbine in the other. John Towns was a retired reporter who came in part-time to do court reporting. He had started work with Blaggs as a boy, at a time when a local journalist learned his trade first by sweeping the office, then by making the tea and finally by acquiring meticulous shorthand. Ellen Atherton was the only woman reporter, waiting to gain her journalistic proficiency certificate, for the completion of indentures, marriage and removal to her fiancé's new home town. Tom Forsyth, on the other hand, had moved north to Blackville from another local weekly newspaper and found life in the north congenial. He was a downwardly mobile ex-public schoolboy of twenty-two and had recently married.

The chief photographer, Ben Field, was a frequent visitor to the reporters' room. He was a fervent vegetarian and a Powellite. Despite his health-giving diet he weighed about sixteen stone, and being short in stature he gave the appearance of having a very large sea-mine secreted under his woolly jumper. Field's visits to the reporters' room were twofold in purpose: to fix up jobs which required both a photographer and reporter; and to argue with the reporters about politics.

Radcliffe and Peters ate together while Ellen Atherton and Tom Forsyth lunched in either the Bowling Green or the Great Northern with reporters and a photographer from the *Gazette* and a reporter from a local freelance agency. Fred Maxwell ate his lunch either at home or in the works with the printers. During much of the working day the office was emptied of most of the staff who were out on stories. Working to deadlines they quickly cleared their notebooks of work on returning. In slack periods the gossip and banter showed the staff to be in relationships of shifting alliances and antagonisms. Apart from the friendship between Peters and Radcliffe, there was frequent evidence of antagonism between reporters and subs. Ellen, Fred and Bertram would join in gossip and mocking while Tom usually limited himself to laughing in support. The most universally disliked member of the subs' room was Williams, who was regarded as unpleasant in his manner, and as bureaucratic and ambitious. Tales of incompetence, domestic misery and illnesses were told with relish. Bill Bradley was the least disliked. Peters was regarded with something short of admiration. He had only recently become a sub-editor after having been regarded by Fred, Ellen and Bertram as an inferior reporter. They also felt Peters's new role was going to his head; he was becoming superior. The significant theme in the criticism of Bradley and Peters was the relationship to Williams; they were allegedly becoming like him.

Both Peters and Bradley on the other hand came into the reporters' room during slack periods for a friendly gossip. This often involved running down Williams. This was regarded by the four 'hard core' reporters with some cynicism. When Tony Radcliffe was in the room no one criticized Peters. Radcliffe was liked, but with some reservations. He tended to forget to tell people which job they were down for and to leave the office without saying where he had gone. When Bertram Guest took over he was conscientious in avoiding these errors. This did not earn him immunity from the slings and arrows of his colleagues, however. Those immune from criticism were Fred Maxwell, Ellen Atherton, Tom Forsyth and John Towns: all of them groundlings untainted by managerial authority.

The allegiances and antagonisms which manifested themselves were related to departmental distinctions. This was exacerbated by the fact that while it was plain what responsibility certain statuses carried in the organization their power over the occupants of other statuses was ambiguous in form and hardly at all apparent in practice. When either Williams, Bradley or Peters came in to ask the meaning of a phrase or offer an alternative mode of expression, this was often taken as criticism and resented. Antagonism was heightened by the fact that the *Examiner* was a 'personality' paper. Reporters were given by-lines on features which they 'worked up' themselves. This had the advantage of providing a supply of predictable editorial material in a 'bright' form. But it also meant that the reporters were committed in a personal sense to the material. The subs on the other hand, had a personal responsibility for their own pages and equally wanted to put their own stamp on their work. There were rival claims on the cachet attaching to a good product and rival interpretations as to what constituted a good product.

To systematize what has been said so far:

Technology	*Organization*	*Interaction*
New offset-printing machinery: resulting in less flexibility because of full use to pay off cost.	bureaucratic corporation:	(1) high predictability of features means reporters work independently;
	(1) maximum use of capital expenditure incurred in take-over;	
	(2) two papers in production;	(2) in order to carry out their specialization, subs need to interfere with reporters' work;
	(3) tight work schedules;	
	(4) accountability to Macro-Type;	(3) inter-departmental antagonism follows;
	(5) managerial division of labour and increased administration;	(4) tension between reporters' autonomy and supervision by formally higher status employees;
	(6) negotiated relations with central office.	(5) internal cohesion of strictly non-managerial reporters.

This is not to suggest that the antagonisms and cohesion sprang from technological factors. Far from it, for technological, organizational and interactional variables are in a mutually interacting relationship. But the form of the organization appears to be the crucial factor, determining the use to which technology was put and the end results to which the technology was geared.

Departmental interaction

One of the objects of inter-departmental friction was the office car, which had been bought for reporters and photographers to drive to jobs. This was taken on a number of occasions by Williams and more frequently by Peters to go out on a job or to go to lunch. Indirect accusations were then countered by allegations that it was the advertising department that had taken it – which had been the case on several occasions. This would be followed by abuse of the advertising departmental reps, who rarely visited the reporters' room. Although there was antagonism between the journalistic sub-departments, they enjoyed a solidarity against what any editorial member construed as a threat from outside. This was reflected in a lack of territorial exclusivity among the editorial workers. It was quite acceptable for one reporter to sit in another's chair while he was out of the room, and when the owner returned and found his place occupied he would simply sit elsewhere. Sometimes one of the reporters would go into Plowden's room to work, if it were empty. Subs would come and sit in the reporters' room, reporters would sit in the subs' room. There was none of the systematic, status-based exclusivity and formality of Littletown. All interaction was on the basis of first names or more familiar terms. In the absence of any attempt to structure the organization around the need for status demarcation, restraints and constraints on behaviour were much laxer.

The impression which the day-to-day working of the editorial department gave was that of a self-regulating mechanism. Rarely did anyone give or receive overt explicit instructions. Each reporter had his own area and produced his own features. Maxwell, especially because of his age, force of personality and knowledge of the area was left much to his own devices. Only as the last front-page dead-line approached did Williams come in and ask 'Two par. stories people, please'. And Williams also sometimes gave orders to Ellen (the only junior, and the only woman), reprimanded her for inadequate work and asked her to make the tea; all of which she resented.

The ability, and the need of reporters to initiate their own work, meant that they dealt directly with contacts, while for their part Williams and the subs, involved with their jobs of presentation, preparation and putting together the paper, were not drawn into contact with the public. Williams especially was also drawn into the organizational aspects of the paper's production and, through Ransom, with the Macro-Type bureaucracy. Whereas at Littletown Debrett went through the council minutes, dealt with contacts and sometimes wrote stories himself, at Blackville council minutes were passed directly to reporters. Each reporter decided on the news-worthiness of their content. If he turned in nothing from a council meeting that was unquestioned. His professional judgement was the final one.

A stinking hole

A number of events illustrate the relatively autonomous role of the reporter and its effect on relations with news contacts. The first simply illustrates how a 'good story' was structured in the organi-zation of the Blackville office. Guest, in charge temporarily of the reporters' room, was given a letter by Williams, who asked if there was anything the reporters could make of it. The letter was from a neighbour of one Aggie Evans who complained that this ancient lady was living in a house which was in a disgraceful condition because of structural neglect. Aggie Evans was old and sick and could not cope. The house had been condemned by the council, which as it happened was also the landlord. Guest decided this would make the basis of a good piece on the theme of the individual against authority.

He took a photographer and went to interview Mrs Evans. They returned with pictures and details of Mrs Evans's abode. She had a semi-invalid son in late middle age who did nothing to keep the house in order. Guest mentioned in recounting his visit that one of the problems was sheer dirt, which was not kept down either by the son or the invalid mother. First and foremost, however, he was outraged by the landlord's neglect, which he saw as the basic cause of this lady's distress. This view found instant support with Ellen Atherton and Fred Maxwell.

It being Tuesday, Williams came in to inquire if anyone had a front-page lead. Guest said the Aggie Evans's letter would make one; Williams accepted this assurance and returned to his layouts. A photograph was produced. It showed a fat old woman sitting blotchy-legged in her filthy, damp sitting-room by her crumbling fire-place. Bradley and Peters wanted to put up the headline 'Aggie Evans's Stinking Hole', which brought peals of laughter. Guest's story was written 'strong', verging on comment. Williams said it was a good one and set it up with a bold, 'strong' headline.

After publication Maxwell was on the phone to James Kilkenny, chairman of the Junior Chamber of Commerce. Kilkenny was a young businessman and they were discussing a story about a new hotel. He was a keen believer in a clean up Blackville campaign and a new image for the north. Maxwell was on first-name terms with Kilkenny and had recently written a number of articles on the JCC's charitable efforts for the elderly. Kilkenny complained that Aggie Evans let down Blackville and ruined the efforts of the JCC. Maxwell disagreed. Kilkenny said Aggie Evans and her son were the kind of people who let the north down. They lived in dirt because they were dirty. Maxwell became angry, invoking truth, brotherhood and equality on behalf of the oppressed woman and the *Blackville Examiner*. The conversation ended with Maxwell fixing up a further interview with Kilkenny in his hotel.

The writing of this story and the unconcern over the subsequent complaint made by Kilkenny about Maxwell's outburst are illustrative of how little the editor interposed himself in the interaction between reporters and contacts. In Maxwell's case his knowledge of the area was such that the possible loss of one contact was easily overcome. And in any event contacts appeared to accept that Maxwell had strong opinions and those such as Kilkenny who had an interest in obtaining publicity continued to provide him with information.

The photogenic urinals

Here is another example of the way in which a reporter exercised his autonomy in writing a news feature article. Again it concerns the JCC, which had undertaken a survey of the public lavatories of Blackville. Its report was sent to the *Examiner* and Guest was asked by Williams to do a feature, with photographs, on Blackville's public gents. Half-jokingly Guest suggested he might visit all the men's public lavatories in Blackville and give them a star rating on the same basis as the Automobile Association's hotel rating. The criteria would be washing facilities, cleanliness, functioning or non-functioning of cisterns, provision of pedestals and so on. Accordingly he set off with the photographer to find Blackville's true-loo position. After a morning of toilet testing he returned to make his report. He produced his own rating and account of each toilet along with the assessment in the JCC report. One of the photographs used was of Guest himself standing in a urinal in the act of carrying out his inspection. At first glance it would have been easy enough to conclude he was urinating. This was Peters's idea. The whole report was used as a full-page feature, laid out and sub-edited by Peters.

Apart from the original request by Williams to Guest to do a feature on the public gents of Blackville the story went through every stage in its production process without being affected by a person occupying a formal managerial status.

Workers' control

The control over the job, which the reporters exercised, involved them in relationships with actors outside the formally demarcated boundaries of the *Blackville Examiner*. This was in the matter of 'doubling up' on stories with other reporters. It was ironic that while Ransom was persuading Macro-Type that it would be against the best interests of the *Examiner* and the *Evening Gazette* to use the same reporters for councils and courts, such a system – as already noted – was already in operation. However, it differed from what Macro-Type wanted to impose both in regard to the categories of reporters involved and in the ideological *raison d'être* and the manner of its operation.

First, the Macro-Type proposals were that a reporter from either the *Evening Gazette* or the *Examiner* should send reports to both papers. The reporters' scheme was that when two reporters were covering the same meeting one would leave and the other stay so that the reporter who left could extend the amount of free time he had. Second, the reporter was not chosen on the basis of whether or not he worked for Macro-Type but on how he behaved in terms of the group of Blackville journalists. Some were regarded as not being fit for help at all, others were helped on a tit-for-tat basis, and the well liked were helped without calculation of specific reward. But all were excluded from being helped with certain kinds of story.

Basically the normal method of doubling up was that one reporter would ring up and ask who was covering court, Blackville Education Committee or whatever the story was and ask his colleague to cover for him, or the request would be made at the meeting. The reporter who stayed would then ring up or meet the other in the pub and read from his own notes the cases or issues which were newsworthy. After that, the other had to do whatever following up, interviewing and lobbying were necessary himself and write up his own story. Now the extent to which the service extended to this level of keeping an eye on the whole proceedings depended on how well the two journalists knew one another. Certain kinds of 'scoop', for instance, based on background knowledge related to council minutes, would not be passed on to anyone. Other kinds of story would depend for their availability on the person making the request. Someone who was a well-known, well-liked reporter with a reputation for straight dealing would get an account of all the possible newsworthy items. Someone less well known would be safe in asking 'Would you mind keeping an eye on X case for me?', but would not be as likely to get a full run-down on stories other than those actually requested. One *Evening Gazette* reporter, Morris Brosnan, was alleged to have been at a council meeting with Ellen Atherton and to have deliberately dissuaded her from using a story on the grounds that it was not worth bothering with. Brosnan had then used the story himself. This was felt to be a particularly underhand trick to play on a less experienced junior, and when Brosnan rang up one day and asked if the reporter covering the court would keep an eye open for stories of interest to him, Maxwell refused to help. On another occasion, Tom Forsyth went to a council meeting where Higgins, the *Herald* reporter, asked him to keep an eye on things. During the course of the meeting an unexpected rent protest by council tenants took place. Forsyth decided not to give this information to Higgins, for the reason that he doubted if Higgins would do as much for him.

The reporter whom the Blackville reporters were most ready to help did not work for the Macro combine. She was Winnie Lees, who worked for one of the local news agencies for less than the NUJ rate. She was struggling to pass her 'O' levels in order to be accepted by the union, and because of her assiduous application and good shorthand always had a 'good note' in court cases. She was willing to help out whenever she was asked and the Blackville reporters were similarly ready to help her. This was also partly because they felt sympathetic towards her on account of the low wages she received and the sweatshop conditions she worked under.

The practice of doubling up elucidates a number of points about the reporters in Blackville, and the relationship between the role which they defined for themselves and that which was defined for them by Macro-Type. First, reporters identified themselves as professionals not simply in relation to the union or some abstract notion of occupational 'norms', or loyalty to the 25,000 other journalists in the country, but in an immediate, active way with a number of visible, accessible actors in their own locality. Second, this identity was associated with a reciprocity of deeds, or a perceived willingness to reciprocate deeds. It would be wrong to regard this as 'a group' or a single system of exchange: except in the sense that there was a dichotomy between the 'ins' and the 'out'. But at the boundary a reporter like Higgins was 'in' only inasmuch as he was seen to be likely to reciprocate. Third, this perception of willingness was the outcome of interaction both as workers engaged on the same jobs and socially during lunch-time and evening drinking sessions and parties. What this meant in relation to involvement with Macro-Type was that in certain areas of role-playing the Blackville reporters disregarded the formal organizational boundaries of Macro-Type. Within the confines of the office the departmental boundaries were accepted, *de facto*, as the criteria for task allocation as between reporters and subs. These were areas of activity controlled by the dominating bureaucratic device employed by the combine – the work schedule. But in the enactment of the reporter's role this schedule only really bit at two points: the allocation of specific jobs to the reporters in preparing the weekly work schedule; and the time of the handover of the reporter's part of the processed product to the sub. What happened between these two points of contact was very much in the control of the individual reporter acting out his role both as a member of a partially autonomous system of communication and in interaction with other reporters and with his contacts.

At this point it should be noted that the reporters disavowed identity with Macro-Type and claimed to a man that they did not feel the company intruded on them greatly. Inasmuch as it did, and inasmuch as it was visibly manifested in the large increase in administrative and advertising staff, they felt it was an unnecessary intrusion into the working of the *Examiner*. This view of theirs was built on a sort of folklore, the idea of a golden past which, they felt, had characterized the *Examiner* in its independent days when everyone had 'mucked in' and worked together as a team. It was a view that involved a universal admiration of and loyalty to Ransom as a manager. It had been imbibed by Ellen Atherton and Tom Forsyth largely from Fred Maxwell, Bertram Guest and Ben Field and given substance by the easy-going camaraderie which seemed to the two newcomers to exist among the reporters. They projected backwards what they regarded as the good points of working life at the *Examiner* and identified the bad points partly with the take-over and partly with Mike Williams's rise to eminence – which was also seen as interconnected with the change in membership and organization.

The limits of control

Before leaving this examination of the relationship between reporters and office journalists at the *Examiner* we shall investigate the sort of things which happened at the boundaries of areas of competence. It is probably significant that the first incident involved Ellen Atherton. Partly because she was a junior and partly because she was a woman she was more amenable to Williams's correctives and as a junior she was still learning where the boundaries intruded. The more experienced reporters had already acquired the necessary manners of occupational behaviour and were able to apply them without questioning. The case in point concerned the question of suitability of material for publication, where a reporter's view is challenged by the deputy editor and where a clear definition of task allocation is identified.

Ellen Atherton had been to a rates tribunal hearing. After the hearing a group of owner occupiers complained to her about their case. They had applied for rates reductions on their houses because of industrial development which they claimed spoilt their amenities. The results of these tribunals are not announced at the hearings but are sent later by post to interested parties, so that Ellen Atherton's story would simply have been an account of the transactions of the inquiry. However, the house-owners' complaint was that they had been swindled by the speculator builder who sold them the houses. They had not been told that the site was already overlooked by a vast power station and itself overlooked a grimy 'flash' and that there was a risk of subsidence from undermining by the coal board.

When Ellen Atherton returned to her office she wrote up the story primarily on the basis of her interviews with the residents and only secondarily mentioned the hearing as a contextual background locating the complaints to some specific event. She wrote that 'angry residents' of the —— estate had alleged they had been misled by the builder who sold them their houses. They had moved to the area from Liverpoool and had been sold the houses on the basis of drawings and architects' impressions.

After she gave Williams the story he read it and came back into the reporters' room, put it on Atherton's desk and uttered the two-word rejection, 'No good'. She asked Williams why he was not going to use it, but he did not elaborate on his verdict. What seemed all too evident was that Williams did not wish to use the story because it libelled the builder and contained statements which might affect the market price of the houses of residents who were not among the protesters – statements which, unlike those made at the tribunal, would not be privileged.

Later on, Maxwell and Peters were discussing the story with Ellen Atherton and commenting on the dishonesty of the builder whom they apparently knew by name. When Williams came into the room, Maxwell commented, 'You didn't use Ellen's story on the jerry-builder then?' Williams repeated his original verdict. He appeared to take a pride in not explaining his decision, although the reasons for his reticence were not hard for the seasoned reporters to surmise. The issue was not a remarkable one, and it is unlikely that an experienced journalist would have submitted such a story on the basis of unsubstantiated statements. Williams must have been well aware that his refusal to use the story would not impress any of the reporters as being based on his individual judgement. He was simply applying the rules as he was supposed to as deputy editor, acting within the formal boundaries of tasks allocated outside the areas of competence laid down for reporters.

The second incident shows an area of ambiguity in task allocation,

and a marked difference in this respect from the practice followed
in the *Littletown Independent*. Ellen Atherton had written a court
story involving a criminal charge against a Mr Ellis of Coke Street;
the 'style' at the *Examiner* was to use only street names without
numbers. However, there were two unrelated men of the same name
in Coke Street. The second Mr Ellis telephoned to complain that his
neighbours thought it was he who had been in court. Ellen Atherton
explained that the Ellis involved had a different first initial and that
this was quite clear in the story. Mr Ellis the second was in no way
mollified by this intelligence and said he would sue for defamation
unless an apology was forthcoming. Ellen Atherton asked him to
hold the line while she got in touch with the editor. She asked
Williams to speak to Ellis and he asked her what the complaint was.
When she explained he told her to tell the caller that the editor would
write to him.

Ellen Atherton did what she had been asked and Mr Ellis rang off
after repeating his threat to sue unless an apology were forthcoming.
No apology was printed nor was a letter sent acknowledging Mr
Ellis's complaint. No further action was taken by Ellis, as, indeed,
there was none he could take.

Two other complaints of a similar type were also dealt with by
reporters without the editor being involved. It seems that this was
the classic mode of dealing with complaints in a bureaucratically
organized newspaper. Drawn into the organizational maelstrom
by the specialized nature of his own work, the editor avoided contact
with news sources and anyone making a complaint. The tactic of
telling the reporter to say the editor would do something meant the
reporter could deal with the complaint while not seeming to take
responsibility, while the editor seemingly took responsibility without
actually doing anything. This situation was still more depersonalized
by a bland statement by Ellen Atherton that it was not the *Examiner*'s
practice to give home numbers, as if her role were simply that of an
impartial technician applying the abstracted house rules.

The bureaucratization of the Examiner

The tactic described above was part of the 'bureaucratization' of
the work organization at Blackville which had two broad effects:

(a) The imposition upon the paper's operation of a specialized
     category of administrators, both at Blackville and at Macro's
     central office, who laid down the ends, the means and the
     distribution of values of the newspaper.
(b) The reorganization of the journalistic work of the office on
     the lines of efficiency in terms of (1) rationalistic accountancy

and (2) in job demarcation reminiscent of scientific management, which take the form of:

(i) the division of labour in managerial tasks. The editor's
role was now split into different functions; allocation of jobs,
sub-editing; laying out pages, combining editorial work and
marrying editorial to advertising, printing and administrative
work;

(ii) the division of the journalist department into two
separate sub-departments:

(iii) the institution of departmental boundaries in the
production process;

(iv) the regulation of journalistic work to fit a bureaucratic
schema.

These developments show the rule-orientated nature of the new
work methods at the *Examiner*. As in Weber's model of bureaucracy
there is 'the principle of fixed and jurisdictional areas;[1] the management of the office is based upon written documents'. The management of the office involves expert training or the fruits of management science and the 'management of the office follows general rules,
which are more or less exhaustive and which can be learned'.[2] The
crucial difference here between the *Independent* and the *Examiner*
is that the few explicit rules at Littletown were not central to the
production process but were simply based on the personal choice of
Reginald Wright, not in relation to a commercial end but as an end
in themselves.

There were two important points at which the operation of the
Blackville Examiner office departed from the bureaucratic model.
First, in relation to the principle of jurisdictional areas, 'the
authority to give commands required for the discharge of these
duties' was *not* 'distributed in a stable way'[3] not 'strictly delineated
by rules concerning the coercive means at the disposal of officials'.
Relatedly, although there was an 'office hierarchy of levels of graded
authority'[4] this did not produce 'a firmly ordered system of super
subordination in which there is supervision of the lower offices by
the higher ones'.[5] In other words, although the other trappings of
ordered systematic administration existed at Blackville, they were
not in a one-for-one relationship with behaviour. The system of
organization left within itself wide areas of ambiguity. And this
ambiguity was an area of competition for power.[6]

Management 'structure' and interaction

Let us examine in more detail the relationship between the formal
managerial structure and actual interaction. Ransom was formally

general manager and was supposed to see to it that the production of the *Blackville Examiner* was undertaken according to Macro-Type rules. But there were two kinds of ambiguity which inhered in his position: (a) there were personnel whose position gave them links with Macro-Type which bypassed Ransom; (b) Ransom because of his control over local communication channels stemming from historic involvement, was able to conduct certain affairs at Blackville without surveillance by Macro-Type.

(a)   This first type of ambiguity related to:

(i)   groups of workers such as printers and journalists who were in 100 per cent unionized situations. Their wages were negotiated at a national level with basic rates settled between their unions and the employers' representatives, and the 'house agreements' between Macro-Type and the unions of the newspaper chain. Ransom was therefore relieved from any collective bargaining responsibility and freed from a source of antagonism. He referred to an overtime ban by the printers as a result of national negotiations as if he were talking about an unfortunate mishap which had befallen the *Examiner* in general and 'our chaps' (the printers) in particular. This only added to his already remarkable popularity.

(ii)   categories of workers whose responsibility was directly to Macro-Type were in effect Snow and his financial assistants. They were identified by the reporters as interlopers who had not been there in 'the golden past'. Even the left-wingers Ellen Atherton and Fred Maxwell expressed loyalty to Ransom and approved of him as an all-round man as opposed to the blue-suited intruder. And inasmuch as Ransom converted Snow to their 'old ways' they rejoiced.

In both respects then this element of ambiguity led to Ransom's being drawn more into identification with Blackville and a sort of nostalgic ideology. Ironically it seemed that the superimposition of the identifiable enemy on to the situation led to the sort of Durkheimian or Elton Mayo-esque[7] solidarity which functionalist orthodoxy would have predicted at Littletown.

(b)   this control over local communication enabled Ransom to expand his capital investments without giving remission, to resist the 'streamlining' of reporters' services. This he could do by capitalizing on his popularity, which was the greater because he used it to thwart Macro-Type.

Relations between Williams and Plowden illustrate how the formal hierarchy of statuses at Blackville was open to renegotiation, through simply not acting out the formally defined statuses. In looking at this relationship we shall again employ the notion of a role as a complex of tasks and of directed ambiguity. It seems evident, looking at the roles of editors both at Littletown and Blackville, that within a role there were both high- and low-status tasks. Status, it appears, is imparted to a role by the enactment of these high-status tasks, so that where an editor enacts, for instance, the task of bargaining with contacts, this raises his status relative to that of a reporter, and gives him power to delimit the reporter's role in the production process. Whereas, when a reporter exercises this task as at Blackville, it gives him power over himself as a worker – viz. autonomy.

As against the unsegmented role of the editor-manager at Out Town we can distinguish a number of features of the fractionalization of the editor's role at Blackville.

The first and most marked feature of this process was the introduction of the new tasks as part of the editorial role. There were the operation of work schedules, the supervision of the new specialization of journalistic roles into the subs and reporters, and negotiations with Ransom over his negotiations within Macro-Type. All of these tasks were undertaken by Williams. He had made himself acquainted with the new type of work organization while Plowden appeared ready to free-wheel downhill to his retirement. In order of their relationship to power and status it seems that negotiating with Ransom was the most important of editorial tasks. Asked anything about the editorial department Ransom would often refer the inquirer to Williams. He also referred to the fact he and Williams were discussing future plans for expanding the office space available to the editorial department. Williams accrued legitimacy from this recognition. This enabled him more convincingly to hand out instructions to subs and to Radcliffe and to initiate changes in the paper's style. The operation of the work schedules was basically only a progress-chasing task, but nonetheless it did seem to involve Williams again in the role of the overseer – the passer-on of instructions, and involved him in this stance more frequently than the less obtrusive tasks already referred to. It had the side effect of self-advertisement as the man in charge. All three tasks were mutually supportive. Ransom listened to Williams because Williams had the day-to-day running of affairs in his hands. The reporters accepted Williams, however reluctantly, because he had Ransom's ear.

Closely allied to Williams's colonization of these areas of editorial activity was the fact that he had undertaken certain of the less high-status tasks of the editor's role, especially during Plowden's illness. These were taking over the layout which Plowden had formerly done, and checking on the progress of stories. Under the new system this was part of operating the schedules, but it was a task which had existed in a more haphazard way beforehand. It also existed at Littletown where it was Debrett's province, although at times he might exercise it through Southall.

Basically this left Plowden with laying out and writing his leader page and receiving a briefing as to what Williams was doing, which in terms of its utility to the production was no more than ritualistic. At some point delegation had become abdication. The role could not be enacted except through control over the tasks. Once the high-status tasks and the low-status tasks, mutually supportive as they were, were amalgamated, Williams was accepted as *de facto* editor by reporters, by Ransom and by the other departmental managers as the man in charge of the editorial department. This invites us to challenge the viability of the notion of fixed jurisdictional areas as if they exist as spaces into which actors stepped without changing the nature of the boundaries. Goldthorpe and Lockwood[8] identify the bureaucratic orientation to work as characterized by an aim to succeed within the terms of the corporation hierarchy. This seems to be a legitimate interpretation of the Weberian bureaucrat. But unless we assume the existence of a pure, altruistic official whose commitment to organizational ends makes him want to succeed, we have to accept that a functionary in the system succeeds by making himself remarkable in some way, either by extra zeal in following the rules or as a man who bends them in order to get the job done.

In the case of Williams, he gave effect to his ambition by bending the formal definition of roles. He stepped into the vacuum created by Plowden's decline and made himself editor, and in so doing changed the roles of editor and deputy editor. Thus, in the event of Plowden's retirement, any new editor would have to cope with Williams in a powerfully entrenched position as the enactor of given tasks in the eyes of the other actors involved. By becoming *de facto* editor he had made it probable then that he himself would take over. But the roles would not remain the same as they were in the incumbency of Plowden and Williams. There is no reason to believe that Williams would relinquish any of his personal power; the likelihood then being that the new deputy editor would effectively have little control at all.

Interaction with contacts

There was now a large area of journalistic activity subsumed under a bureaucratic mode of production and administration. One area, however, remained intractable to this sort of process: relations between reporters and contacts. The presentation of the *Blackville Examiner* as a personality paper with by-line features increased the predictability element but could not obviate such needs in the collection of hard news for the front page. This task could only be accomplished through the co-operation or acquiescence of actors who were not within the control of the bureaucratic regulation of Macro-type. At Blackville these actors were dealt with by reporters. Negotiations were conducted and bargains arrived at not by the deputy editor but by the reporters. Indeed, the deputy editor shunned such contact. He took no active part in community affairs outside work, and at work, apart from writing the very occasional story, he avoided any direct commitment other than those within the ambit of administratively defined activities. Involvement with contacts at work or outside it might well have resulted in pressures and negotiations which would have interfered with his enactment of the corporation drama. Williams left the reporters to get on with their job and only became interested in their work when it was past the stage of being raw material.

The reporters in their turn enjoyed a high regard for their own efficacy. They did not suffer from the downward-role ambiguity which restricted the reporters at Littletown. They operated their own methods of work, at times with other reporters from other organizations. They operated a linage business. Fred Maxwell, for instance, and Tony Radcliffe were paid retainers as sports reporters by a news agency and used the *Examiner* office as a base for their activities. And in between Mike Williams and the reporters were the sub-editors. Their job involved them in correcting reporters' copy and in checking when stories would be available for the pages they were laying out. This involved them in a quasi-managerial relationship with the reporters: but it was not, as we have seen, a relationship to which the reporters acquiesced with any readiness.

Whether or not the subs' job actually included instructing the reporters what to do did not appear to be clear to anyone. The job of the sub-editor was to correct copy, set up the headlines and see to it that his page was laid out in time in accordance with the work

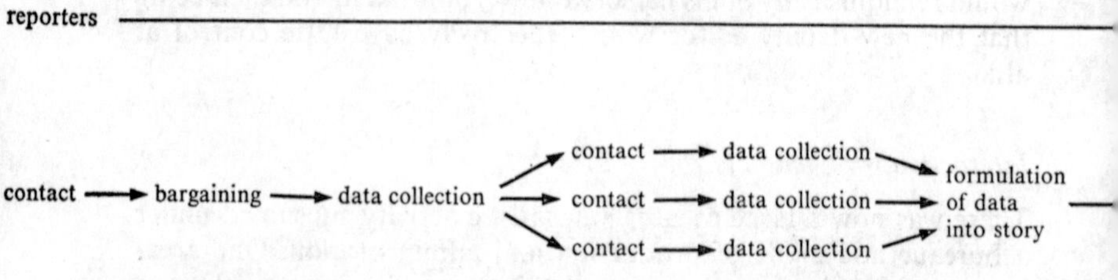

DIAGRAM 3

BLACKVILLE EXAMINER: PRODUCTION OF NEWS STORY/FEATURE

schedules. This whole job, once he had got the copy from the reporter, involved controllable material, whereas for the reporter in news coverage, and even in feature writing to a lesser extent, he was dealing with material that was to a greater or lesser degree unpredictable. But because it was unpredictable and the successful outcome of his activities depended on his exercising skill and judgement, he was not open to close scrutiny. Bradley and Peters on the other hand worked under the direct scrutiny of Williams, and their activities could always be checked against the schedule.

Conclusion

We shall now schematize the patterns of interaction at the *Blackville Examiner* using the same approach as was employed in analysing interaction and power at the Littletown paper. However, because of the greater organizational complexity of the *Examiner* it will be necessary to use a model reflecting more numerous categories of actors.

In looking at the diagrammatic representation of the production of an editorial item at the *Examiner* (Diagram 3) it is apparent that the reporter's areas of competence are clearly delineated. He does not suffer the downward-flowing ambiguity of the Out Town reporter, and the deputy does not interpose himself between the reporter and contacts at various points along the chain of events but takes over at a given point, after which the reporter is finished with his work, unless there is a subsequent complaint, apart from reading it. Where the ambiguity exists in this situation is between reporters and sub-editors at the point of take-over, and between deputy editor and editor.

If the deputy editor/*de facto* editor Williams is not interposed during the process of writing and publishing a story between reporter and contact, this is strongly related to his intra-involvement in a different area of interaction. This is the bureaucratic process in-

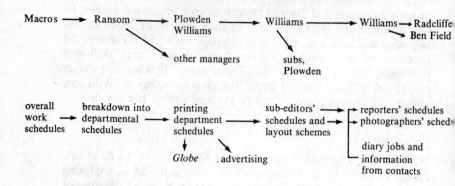

DIAGRAM 4 BLACKVILLE EXAMINER: DOMINANT PARTICIPATION IN EDITOR

volved in matching a newspaper each week to the organizational mould in which the editorial work is formed. In order to see Williams's pervasive participation in these events one must look at the production of the whole editorial content of the newspaper for a given edition. Williams (Diagram 4) interposes himself at a number of crucial points. At the discussions, or reception of instructions from Macro-Type via Ransom, between Ransom and the managers of other departments, Williams is the representative, or at least joint representative when Plowden is included, of the editorial department. He is then the one who takes charge of the drawing up of layout schemes and sub-editing schedules to fit the works manager's time allocations to individual printers. And this seems to be the most crucial stage in organizing the work of the editorial departments. It is Williams who passes on information about these schedules to Plowden.

 Williams is still engaged in certain low-status tasks – sub-editing and working in the printing department – which relate as it were to the carrying out of policy as opposed to its creation. But these enable him to interpose himself further in the production cycle and reinforce his position.

 In both these diagrams an attempt has been made to allow for every possibility. It would be wrong to take them as pictures of regular events. For instance, Macro-Type did not pass on a new

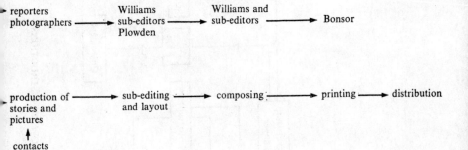

overall work schedule for Ransom each week. But the general work schedule, the sharing of machinery with the *Globe*, periodic changes in deadlines and the like, emanate from Macro-Type, and these set the initial constraint on planning the week's work. As in Diagram 3, it was only occasionally the case that a complaint was received or that a story was rewritten and rarer still that a return was made to a contact by a sub-editor.

Diagram 5 indicates in broad terms the flow of instructions in the production of the *Blackville Examiner*. The greater complexity of role allocation and the bureaucratic nature of the administration in comparison with the *Littletown Independent* are such that any mapping of shifting alliances at the managerial level would be confusing and in any event beyond the scope of the data provided. At the more microscopic level of the reporters' room or the editorial department, a diagram would not add to the verbal account already given.

Williams's nodal position is only partly a reflection of his power. It is also a reflection of the technical nature of his job. In order to do his layouts and get a page out he needs to pass on instructions in the form of requests for work to be done to photographers, printers, van drivers and advertising representatives via their appropriate departmental managers. This nodality may be suppor-

T.S.W.—E

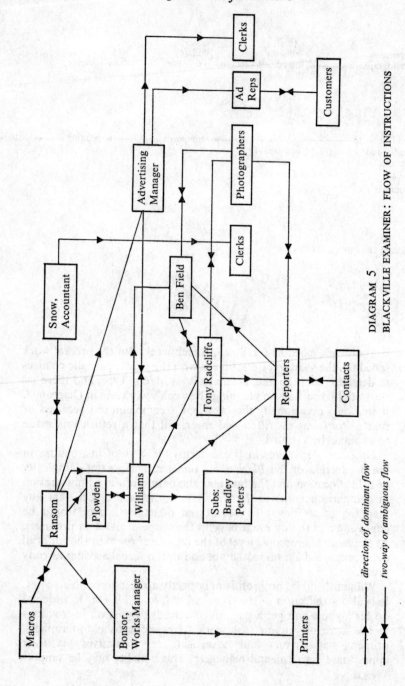

DIAGRAM 5
BLACKVILLE EXAMINER: FLOW OF INSTRUCTIONS

direction of dominant flow
two-way or ambiguous flow

tive of his control inasmuch as he is seen hobnobbing with other high-status actors and in that it gives him access to information, but it does not have a given relationship to power. Snow the accountant, for instance, is largely isolated from the general flow of instructions involved in the production processes. But he has direct contact with Ransom and this relationship, though not equalitarian, is not simply a super-subordination one. Through Ransom, Snow has access to the whole paper. The fact that the Macro rules and the law lay down certain functions as being necessary and that Snow as accountant has the appropriate knowledge and skills, gives him an independent source of power.

In their form and content relationships at Blackville did not manifest the same exclusiveness as at Littletown. Everyone except Ransom was addressed by his first name or a nickname. No one person could claim overall personal responsibility or competence, and no one could lay claim to prerogative of ownership. Superordination was justifiable only by reference to its relevance to the need to get work done by the set deadlines; which was accepted by the reporters as a necessary fact of life. There was no 'pretending to work' at Blackville. Once a reporter's work was done he would sit with his feet up and talk; and no one, neither Ransom nor Williams, ever criticized a reporter for this mode of conduct. So although there was antagonism this was related to given situations: it would probably be expressed in the form of character assassination. But at other times the same actors would be sitting in one another's chairs exchanging anecdotes and cigarettes.

This 'limited liability' to the firm on the part of these employees – even including Williams – was a partial expression of a much more proletarianized editorial work-force. This was probably caused by three factors: the bureaucratic, more 'mass' nature of Macro-Type; the greater preponderance of reporters with working-class backgrounds; the more proletarian nature of Blackville by comparison with Littletown. This proletarianized element of interaction expressed itself in two ways. Reporters and subs were union members and in large part militant. One of the reporters' complaints against subs was that they were weak in support of the union because they thought they were a 'cut above' reporters. This criticism the subs in words and deeds made shift to rebut. The other feature was the evident partial proletarianization of management. The visible management at Blackville – other than the accountant who was considered a Macro-Type company man – were all seen by reporters as in some sense one of them, rather than part and parcel of Macro's. Paradoxically the consent basis of managerial legitimacy at Blackville rested on the common dislike of the organizational structure shared by management and workers.

PART FOUR

Conclusion

7
Conclusions

The notion that there is direct relationship between social effectiveness or political power and possession of information or control
over communication is fashionable in sociological theory.[1] Its
popularity derives at least in part from its validity. The relationships
are complex and are analysed in a variety of ways. Mitchell and
others[2] attempt to refine the concept of the social network as an
element in explaining individuals' effectiveness and their incorpor-
ation in power systems. At a more general level Deutsch analyses
the viability of a political system in terms of its cohesiveness as a
system of communication and the importance of communication
as a source of power.[3] Neustadt[4] shows how lack of adequate information frustrates the ability of the seemingly massively powerful
to guarantee the implementation of their ukases. Bernstein,[5] the
ethnomethodologists[6] and Goffman[7] relate social competence to
possession of knowledge about the appropriateness of forms of
communication in various situations. Goffman, Garfinkel and
McHugh[8] appear to share at some level a common concern with
the exercise of power in interaction through the manipulation of
communication.

These approaches broadly tend to stress positional variables
(e.g. 'network', organizational 'gatekeeper' positions) or qualitative
or structural variables relating to the acts of communication. The
study of the local press and its role in the local 'power structure' has
by and large not confronted the issue of the relationship between
journalistic activity and power. The sociology of mass communication when it has been concerned with such issues has looked at
simple-minded questions: how much control do proprietors exert
over news coverage;[9] how do contacts influence the newspaper;[10]
how do editors exert control over the news they include?[11] Mostly,
however, media sociology has not been overly concerned with such
issues as these but has looked at the victims, those at whom the
media messages are aimed, asking such questions as how much
effect do political campaigns have.[12] The way in which such thinking
reflects the sort of market research-oriented, conservative-estab-
lishment bias with a Mayo-like view of the public as aboriginal hordes
hardly needs stressing.

In order to clarify certain apposite questions, one needs to
elucidate more fully what appears to be lacking in existing communi-

cation studies. First, the images they deal in are static. Breed's questions, for instance, are of this type: does the proprietor exert control over news coverage, yes or no. Breed's issues[13] are almost always amalgams of layers of still silhouettes laid one on top of the other in the manner of silk-screen printing. Are proprietors more liberal or less liberal than newspapermen; are executives more liberal or less liberal than reporters; is the paper's policy Conservative or Liberal; who therefore exerts more influence? Donohew[14] and Carter[15] attempt the same kind of analysis with newspaper gatekeepers.

Second, but associated with the static quality, other analyses combine a rigid organizational view with an almost Taylorite atomism. White[16] and Gieber[17] concentrate heavily on the alleged psychological processes of news editors in selecting news. But they are concerned with the rational stated reasons they gave to sociologists. This is reinforced by the editors they looked at who operated (apparently) in a very isolated way. The explanations are asked for and given in terms and in a manner that answers a sociologist's question; not in a way which would naturally form part of the social process of being a newsman. At the same time the analysis is intra-organizational or accepts as empirically valid the organizational boundaries of the newspaper. (Perhaps this is a reflection of the vocational bias of the academic institutions producing much of the research). It does not put to the test the issues of the nature of organization and the fluidity of perceptions of organizationally relevant boundaries.

The studies rarely use appropriate methods. Frequently it is not only that the images are static. They are also images of issues which are by definition processual and dynamic: power relations; organizational practices; work activities; actors' perceptions. What has struck me repeatedly in my own research, in directly observed situations, is how explanations, rationalizations, accounts of events, change, develop, reverse themselves. Breed uses accounts of events given to him by correspondents as a basis for making judgements about power relations between proprietors and journalists, without questioning the validity of the data.[18]

Probably the most crippling aspect of the traditional studies is their perpetual reliance on the 'gatekeeper' approach. This involves a mummification of relationships so profound that it only really works on isolated individuals. The idea is that certain positions are nodal and therefore the person occupying the position has power over the flow of information. But the use of the model involves the *assumption* that journalists such as wire editors[19] do occupy gatekeeper positions. They do not clarify in what types of organizational flow these positions constitute 'gates'. They do not clarify their criteria of nodality. The fact of nodality and therefore of organizational power is assumed by the analysts. The questions to ask, it seems, are what the criteria of nodality are and how to operationalize these criteria, and then to tackle the considerable problems of how to measure the data in relation to the demands of the model. Mitchell's[20] detailed analysis of the conceptual implications of the network model would constitute a paradigm for the development of network analysis. His account also of the difficulties of quantifying the concept and the impossibility of quantifying the most valuable explanatory variables could be applied with good reason to the related problems of gatekeeper analysis. One solution is certainly not, as White does, to assume that some particular operative is a gatekeeper, and assume away all the conceptual, relational and empirical difficulties at the same time.

A final objection to much sociological analysis of the local media is the acceptance of the organizational ideology of local government and the newspaper proprietors in their identity of the universes of power. Janowitz[21] accepts the local authority as the context within which he studies his Chicago newspapers. Norton E. Long,[22] while adopting a more critical and contingent notion of community, nonetheless looks at the outcome of 'community' processes at the level of the locality defined in terms of newspaper coverage and local government writ. Breed and the other organizational analysts concern themselves with power relations in the newspaper office and ignore the interaction of the personnel with powerful (and powerless) outsiders.

The model within which we shall analyse the process of news gathering is that of continuous and interlinked chains of influence forming a matrix of individuals attempting to pre-empt at various points the actions of other people whom they see as being amenable in some sense to their influence. Their picture of the process rather than the 'nature' of the matrix is the explanatory factor. The matrix itself is like a demand curve in that it can only have validity as an instantaneous picture of events. It is a picture which is constantly changing. It is, like a market situation, neither of necessity in equilibrium or disequilibrium; that depends on the dynamic relation of the parts. If one part changes disproportionally to the rest, either excessively or inadequately, a sector of the matrix may explode or wither. But that does not mean that it cannot be revived, to a greater or less degree of completeness.

Of course, while we might postulate an infinite grid of interaction on to which may be imposed relationships of gossip, power, recorded communication, commercial exchange, and involving sexual interplay, this is not what we are interested in. Rather, we want to look at the particular bit of the grid which our heroes see at any time, especially at the overlaps and at the changes. Mitchell draws attention[23] to the difficulty of calculating one person's social network, simply in terms of counting heads. This seems to me to be a fairly hare-brained endeavour in any case. What is of interest is just who, in an actor's own perceptions, is relevant in a particular context and this, it appears, can only be in terms of the actor's own frame of reference. So although we might regard an infinite matrix of permanent change and contingent stability as a valid model of reality, we need only use as an explanatory device the perceptions and evaluations, in both normative and instrumental terms, entertained by the actor. Let us not concern ourselves with 'reality' if it is beyond the ken of the actors, as an explanation of their conscious acts. What we are looking at then are limited, relevant and personal networks.

Now this may suggest an approach close in many respects to that of ethnomethodology. This is not so. We are concerned with explanation in terms of relationships between different areas of interaction which takes into account the social context; which employs perceptions which cannot be strictly measured or even at times proved to exist by reference to any recording devices; which takes account, where necessary, of social and conversational inflexions which we assess as observers rather than a 'pure' concern with content or sequence; which does not involve rules, constitutive or otherwise;[24] which takes into account 'cultural variables'; and which, hopefully, is capable of forming part of a larger explanation of societal phenomena. On the other hand in common with ethnomethodologists we are concerned with the detailed explanation of social life in terms of the achievements of individual actors and with explanations in terms of normal practices rather than the perpetual fall-back of rationality or some kind of structuralist grand scheme. Further, in attempting to analyse such terms as organization, let us follow Bittner in accepting that the study of 'the methodical use of the concept of organization seeks to describe the mechanisms of sustained and sanctioned relevance of the rational constructions to a variety of objects, events and occasions to which they are invoked'[25] – the spirit of the argument, notwithstanding his crucifixion of English. We should also share the concern of Zimmerman[26] and Cicourel[27] in regarding facts not as entities ascertainable by reference to abstract criteria, but as social achievements. However, even though one does not accept members' 'lay' explanations or common-sense interpretations as analytical frames of reference, on what basis one wonders, do ethnomethodological explanations *generally* enjoy a higher intellectual status than, say, lay members' explanations or even the explanations of structural sociology? The 'facts' of ethnomethodology are just as much social achievements as those of their subject: the 'facts' and analysis that are offered here are certainly not put forward with any pretence of inherent 'scientific' superiority.

Where phenomenologists attempt to analyse the press, the outcome of their efforts looks remarkably like those of straight sociology. Molotch and Lester[28] proceed by painful steps ('an occurrence is any cognized happening' and 'important occurrences demarcate time') to an 'event classificatory scheme' differentiating happenings in relation to the source of their promotion ('effectors' or 'informers') and in the absence or presence of intention. Events then fall under one of four headings: Routine, Scandal, Serendipity and Accident. These are words to describe news stories or 'events' which could have been called out of the air by any 'lay member'. In the case of journalist 'lay members' one hopes they would also do it with more elegance. Gaye Tuckman[29] manages to state the apparently obvious with massive fire-power of an argument by authority. 'News work thrives upon processing unexpected events, events that burst to the surface in some disruptive exceptional (and hence newsworthy) manner' (Noyes, 1971). As Helen Hughes (1940) noted, 'Quickening Agency' is the 'essence of news' (p. 58). Tuckman rejects 'categories' of news as a means of understanding news work and resorts to 'typifications'. Now while it is plain that typifications are claimed to be bedded in the routine achievements of doing journalistic work it is not entirely clear how any startling new understanding arises out of this, no doubt, infinitely significant choice of words. Sigelman's ambiguously entitled effort at an organizational analysis of news reporting[30] turns out to be a return to that theme so beloved of the traditional sociologists from the functionalist Breed onwards: namely the relationship between the political tendencies of the newspaper owner and the political leanings of reporters.

In sum, these studies are bounded by the context of the newspaper office and newspaper activities: lay categories do form the framework for research. They claim to be studies of processes but they fall back on classifications of events, typifications of stories, attitudes of journalists and policies of newspapers: on static categories. Generalized accounts of what newsmen do, with a passing reference to an incident, do not make clear how news arises out of the interaction among journalists and between journalists and actors not constrained by the newspaper's organizational context.

At the same time orthodox analysis of local politics appears to be primarily concerned with attacks on or the defence of the liberal-democratic myth. Idealized, abstract models made up of various interacting elements and depending on evidence about the detailed processes of political interaction are substantiated by second-hand evidence. In the case of the power élite theorists, the 'élite' group's existence is established by the reputational method, and stories

about the group's activities supporting the hypothesis of its existence.[31] On the other hand the pluralist, decision-orientated method
claims to be concerned with the processes but in fact accepts the
formal overt management of conflict as recounted by those committed to the system.[32] It is based upon an iron-bound, simple-minded
Aristotelean model in which there are parties with means and ends
which are apparently related to factual evidence (which appears to
be regarded as unproblematic – except in that it might be difficult to
obtain). Superimposed on to this is the external version of the actors'
means-end dichotomy, namely the cause-and-effect chain. Causes
are political pressure (the actor's means) and the effect is a decision
(which can then be measured against the intended ends of the
actors).[33]

There are objections to both standpoints. The existence or non-
existence of an élite is either a will-o'-the-wisp or a complex statement
about interaction. If the writer propounds a functionalist 'organic'
notion of group it is the former: if on the other hand 'group' is a
shorthand term for a cluster of interaction around given interests
and issues, assuming a level of intensity, and relationships of power,
status, competition and co-operation, then in order to investigate
such a set of phenomena what is required is observation of these
processes: not a second-hand allegation that they exist. Secondly,
the allegation that a powerful group exists in a town is not an
explanation of the nature of political power but a phenomenon
requiring explanation. Further, the observation of political events
is then not put forward simply as an impressionistic support for a
polemic but as a phenomenon *sui generis*, worthy of analysis. But
the data are not to be either (a) second-hand accounts or (b) concentrated around issues defined as relevant by those who operate the
political system. The local government set-up, in other words, does
not define the relevant boundaries for research questions. When the
accounts of actors of past events are not accepted as data about the
past events but as data about the actors, and when the events
themselves are observed, it becomes increasingly plain that the
actors' statements about the past and about their intentions and their
reasons for doing things are subject to constant change as they
attempt to give meaning to events. What are often the 'primary
sources' for academic research – local authority documents and local
newspaper stories – are seen to be the outcome of social processes
which are not simply explained in terms of the structuring of reality
as an ideology but rather as the outcome of competing ideologies.

It is now necessary to add the notion of ideology to the model of a
selected network which is centred both on specific actors and based
on perceived relevance. In order to see how reality is structured out
of a process of interaction it is possible to put forward three types of

situation: that of ideological uniformity; that of ideological competition; that of ideological conflict. In a situation where the network of interaction is small and intense and replicated over a number of areas, as in the case of the Marlborough Drive group, this is likely to lead to ideological uniformity and in consequence to an unmoderated structuring of ideology. Faced with an antagonistic view of events there is no compromise, and conflict is resolved only by recourse to coercion. In all the cases noted here this meant the use of the libel laws or local government secrecy – which seemed to generate both apathy and a confirmation of the conspiracy hypothesis. Ideological competition appeared to characterize those situations where there was a large-scale, open pressure group directed by actors who wished to maintain mass support in order to influence the council. This meant that the aims of the body varied over time. There was a reinterpretation of past aims and therefore, in turn, of past strategies. Activities which were fanfared as the harbingers of great events and boundless success are subsequently hailed as successful if only a fraction of the originally intended result is achieved. Past intentions are then reconstructed – 'This is what we wanted from the outset' – and a new situation with a newly constructed reality exists.

For such a pressure group, accommodation by actors to the rules of competition and the language of other organizations is a precondition to the achievement of political success. Only by setting negotiations in motion can they hope to achieve a compromise, and in order to set such negotiations in progress it is essential to learn the way in which the organizations talk, where they talk and which are the effective personnel to achieve a given result. This requires a flexible approach in which new information can be absorbed into an existing ideology and produce a new position. The council's committee structure and its departmental structure, have to be mastered so that the protesters talk to the relevant people about appropriate issues. The rules of relevance in structuring reality need to be understood – how is a house defined as 'unfit for human habitation'? In talking to newspaper personnel an attempt has to be made to formulate their protest in the form of a 'good story'; account has to be taken of 'big paper days', the best reporter for dealing with particular issues has to be found. At the same time the leaders of such a group structure past events, present events and forecasts in such a way as to underline their own efficacy. 'We are now listened to by the council', 'We got quite a good coverage of our activities', may be the recycling of 'The council met us and basically told us to get lost' and 'We got a single-column, three-inch story in the *Manchester Evening News* and a single par. in *The Guardian*'. This optimistic reinterpretation of events may well lead them to believe that the techniques they are applying are more efficacious than they seem to their victims or targets and that a continued application will only continue to produce modest, if any, success in terms of the aims they themselves have been stating in the past – 'We can lead the way in an experiment in participatory democracy', 'The council must be forced to see that its plans are not acceptable to the people'. If the leaders of a protest cannot persuade the council of its errors then they must use their social skills on their own followers – to cover up defeat, exaggerate victories and generally put a hopeful complexion on events. If the council can spare them sufficient 'face' to achieve this survival, an ordered negotiating structure can be maintained.

Where ideological competition exists there must be differences in ideology only of degree. The pressure group accepts that some houses must be knocked down; the council accepts that some houses can be improved. The pressure group accepts that the traffic problem has to be dealt with; the council accepts that some increased costs in road construction is possible if this is necessary to save some homes. Where such a statement is forthcoming from the council it is presented by the leaders as a victory. Then, if subsequently, the council goes ahead and knocks down half of the village to widen a road, some at least of the pressure-group leadership will be committed, in the interest of portraying themselves as good leaders, to interpreting this as consistent with their earlier undertaking to save houses where possible. The alternative cry of 'We were betrayed' is synonymous with 'We are idiots', and therefore unpalatable.

The newspaper for the reasons outlined in Chapter 1 and subsequently expanded is committed to an image of ideological competition. It is not, like the open pressure group, concerned with the processing of reality into a new orthodoxy in order to gain something out of this competition, but in presenting the competition of arguments itself as an end, thus, though not necessarily by intention, supporting a pluralist democratic view of society and politics. The newspaper, in the interests of the 'good story' and the market, is concerned with content only inasmuch as it fits a certain form. The little man against the bureaucrat is a good story angle. Bureaucrats are insensitive, inefficient, legalistic, against sex and pets in flats are all legitimate themes for the 'little man against the bureaucrat' story. Bureaucrats are thieves, swindlers, cover up swindling by politicians, run the system for their own personal economic benefit are only good topics when they are court reports. This is not only because of the libel laws; it is also because the newspaper has to report something which is happening. Hard news or good news, especially at the level of the local weekly, is not 'X road is in a derelict condition'. But on the other hand 'Fifty householders threaten rates strike because of the derelict condition of X road' is certainly hard news. Something is happening and the newspaper cannot be held to account for initiating anything. When the press carries a local corruption case as a court report it is simply providing an account of the system correcting its own faults. No unpleasantness such as refusal of co-operation by contracts is likely to follow. In other words it is responding passively to the stimulus of 'the system'.

None of this is to say that newspaper organization or technology or the market causes a certain approach in the journalist's construction of reality. It is the *journalist's perception* of phenomena which may be categorized under these headings which defines the limits on his behaviour. The involvement by the deputy editor Williams in the chain of newspaper's bureaucratic organization led to the reporters' controlling the flow of information between the newspaper and contacts and being able to control their own work methods. Williams's zealous application of the deadlines led to the stress on predictability and control. In general the coverage of news being oriented to control over cost is not the operation of an impersonal market, but the result of the *editor's interpretation* of values based on market considerations. In other words no super-personal, social organism is being called into service to explain behaviour. But inasmuch as explanations are being formulated in terms of individual ideologies, perceptions etc., it is also necessary to acknowledge that individuals are constrained by social and technological factors. If you pour lead into a Webb offset printing machine or send messages in Chinese to Macro-Type head office you are not likely to succeed long as a local newspaper editor.

The intention here is to show how individuals in organizations (which are collectivities of other individuals acting out parts) constrain and direct their behaviour in order to succeed or survive in that environment; and how the organization also provides them with levers and strategies in the competitive struggle for survival.

The local authority is geared both to ideological competition and to ideological uniformity, which generates conflict when faced with external threat. This makes for complex relationships with the press and local protest groups. Obviously in an institutional sense the local government system provides the substance and framework of ideological competition between the political parties. This is legitimized by the officials and politicians and when it is reported in the press the notion is that democracy is being done and being seen to be done. In a sense, when a newspaper reports council debates it acts as an arm of the local establishment.[34] There is a further sense in which a local authority is overtly geared to ideological competition. Certain local pressure groups come to be accepted as having legitimate claims to consultation in given areas of governmental activity. Ratepayers' associations or trade councils may have their opinions sought on such matters as proposals for parking bans or traffic management schemes. In other areas protests may be regarded as legitimate when coming from a newly formed source. A group of residents may organize a protest over the smell from a nearby sewage works, as a result of which the local authority officers are likely to organize a meeting to negotiate a solution. Covertly there is likely to be interdepartmental competition over policies. For instance, it was widely believed in the 1971–72 period that there was a marked disagreement in Manchester Town Hall between the planning department and the health department over the stress which was placed on clearances, the planning department favouring increasingly the use of improvement areas, the health department adhering to its ancient orthodoxy of laying large areas of the city waste and then loosing gargantuan redevelopments into these Siberian steppes of brick-ends and isolated pubs.

However, at the level of official generation of policy either prior to or outside the consideration of the elected members, local government manifests a rigid uniformity whose chief characteristic is secrecy. Any covert policy differences between departments are hidden by bland statements emanating from officials. Two sorts of document usually issue forth from the council bureaucracy: minutes and correspondence. As we saw in Chapter 3 minutes may be written in such a way as not to convey anything specific and at the same time not indicating where certainty and doubt exist. The use of the passive voice, 'it was agreed', of adverbs of time, 'previously', 'subsequently', instead of dates, referring to actors by general categories, 'the owner', instead of by name, leads to a version of language which is an extreme form of Bernstein's 'formal language'[35] in which qualification and complexity result in an almost total attenuation of meaning. The journalist's 'good story' is typified by 'hard' facts or 'good talking point' controversy, in relation to which the council-minute language stands at exactly the opposite pole.

One of the cries of anguish from editors and those concerned with the training of young journalists is the tendency of juniors and even more experienced reporters to fall into local governmentese when creating stories from the council minutes. What they are expected to do by the seniors is:

(a) To rewrite the items in 'plain English', which simply means paraphrase in a more athletic form of language, with short sentences, few subordinate clauses, in which preferably the introduction is either:

(i) a summary of the whole story and the remainder an expansion of this; or

(ii) a 'come hither' (Vicar Ronald Quilge was surprised to wake from an afternoon nap in the vicarage garden at Pules, Somerset, and find himself surrounded by a party of topless waitresses') which is followed by an explanation. In the first form, that associated with 'hard' news, it should be possible to sub from the end: that is, to drop the last paragraph, then the next, and the next, successively, without destroying the central point. The paragraphs are arranged in descending order of importance. Similarly in the second version after the explanatory section the paragraphs descend in their centrality to the theme 'I thought I must be dreaming. The last thing I remembered was reading the *Church Times*', commented Vicar Ron', and similar tailpieces can be cut away without damage to the main anecdotal quality. This means that an editor or sub-editor working fast at the last minute can cut a story to fit a space without reading it, simply telling a compositor to omit the last three paragraphs.

(b) To 'dig out stories' underlying the bland entries in the council minutes: this may mean digging out those pieces of the minutes which say something fairly concrete. Alternatively it may mean ringing up a committee chairman or a council official for an amplification of an item that looks as if it may carry a potentially 'good story'. Digging is not then to be equated with investigating but with a process of finding suitable material for formulation in terms of the 'good story' construct. The basis of this process is a hunt through the minutes fortified by knowledge of the area, experience of the minutes (parish-pump 'Kremlinology') and a response to certain words which may trigger off responses because of their relevance to a given audience. For instance, the case of improvement grants when they were a national issue, which meant that stories related to them transcended the strictly parochial and might be included in the nationally oriented *Guardian* or the *Manchester Evening News*. At the other pole, at the *Littletown Independent*, any local government decision on the quarries, the hospital or historic buildings would be regarded as newsworthy by virtue of its relevance to its *causes célèbres*.

Overall, bearing in mind the passivity of the local press in reporting news, expressed in its reliance on news contacts as sources of information, the secrecy of local affairs constitutes a major blockage in the potential flow of information.

Let us now turn to correspondence. The obvious fact about correspondence from local authorities is not only that it bears the corporate letter heading and a departmental imprimatur, but that it is the responsibility of a particular individual. That individual is of course surviving, successfully presumably, since he is a departmental head, in a bureaucratic environment, and one over which a political stratum exerts an erratic control. If an official oversteps his responsibility, makes a statement to the press, writes a letter to a pressure group giving information away in advance of officially telling the council, or is seen to be pre-empting councillors' powers, he is likely to be attacked by council members. On the other hand officials may as a matter of fact but not in public formulate policies to which councillors acquiesce, perhaps in ignorance of the evidence. Committees make decisions which the council subsequently rubber stamp. But the structure of reality placed on such processes by the law is that no decision has been made prior to the official rubber-stamp vote of the council. So, to take an example, where negotiations are in hand for the sale of a council-owned house, until the officials have put a proposed agreement before one or several committees and the decisions of the committees are approved by the full council, the council may have no formal policy to sell the house. When an occupant of the house writes offering to buy it the official is legally correct in saying that the council has no plans to sell the house, and if negotiations are already in progress or begun subsequently there is no legal responsibility on the part of the officials to tell the occupant; because at that time nothing binding has been done.

Or to take a second example, a sub-committee of the Manchester Education Committee was considering a report by one of its officers involving the reorganization of adult education in one of the city's further education areas. This involved a plan for the eventual phasing out of an adult education centre building which was the only major community building in a depressed working-class area with a large old-age pensioner population. A student at the education centre phoned the education department but was unable to contact the official who had written the report. She then wrote in protest to the education officer: 'It seems rather strange that recommendations made by sub-committees are kept from the interested public until such time as it is impossible to try to alter the recommendations made.'

The official reply, signed by the education officer, countered:

I am sorry you feel aggrieved at being unable to obtain information about the proceedings of sub-committee before these are submitted for confirmation by the Education Committee. This is, however, correct practice and any officer declining to give information about sub-committee decisions would have my full support. These proceedings become public at meetings of the

Education Committee but are themselves subject to confirmation by the City Council at a meeting about two weeks later. There is, therefore, plenty of opportunity to challenge decisions of the Education Committee before they are presented to the City Council. If you have attended any meetings of the City Council you will know that this happens on occasion.

He added that there was nothing in the recommendations going forward to the next meeting of the education committee to indicate that it was proposed to cease activities at the centre.

This indicates two aspects of the response of the bureaucracy, acting strictly to the 'letter of the law'. The first is that whereas at national level the civil service consults with public bodies and pressure groups in the preparation of the 'departmental view', at local level the public is generally excluded. There are no white papers, discussion papers, green papers. There are, in Manchester (and experience elsewhere suggests that this is not rare), reports by chief officers to committees marked always 'Private and Confidential' and not referred to in the published minutes. The report in this case did indicate that the centre was expected eventually to close down, although in his letter the education officer was strictly correct again in saying that there was nothing in the *recommendations* of the *sub-committee* to indicate that it was proposed to cease activities. This is the second aspect: that a response may mean exactly what it says, but may in effect, accidentally or not, screen much of the actual processes of government. It may also be taken to mean something quite different by those for whom qualification of meaning and legalistic precision are alien. In the case in point, the officer's letter might be considered as a reprieve or an undertaking that the centre would be spared.

Now the organizers of protests often rely on such correspondence as one of their sources of information about the circumstances in which they are interested, but even more about the state of mind of the administrators. They are also interested inasmuch as statements by officers might constitute levers for future negotiations. At the same time they usually have additional information from other sources about (a) the facts on which policy is based, such as the condition of houses in clearance areas or the ownership of property, and (b) about the processes of local government, from simply observing council employees with measuring-tapes to having knowledge of internal procedures and even photocopies of maps, and documents from council employees who are well disposed towards the protest group. Of course some beliefs about what the council is up to become distorted; occasional inspections by public health inspectors can be constructed into a conspiracy theory, as we have seen. Men appearing with measuring-tapes at the adult education centre gave rise rapidly to a rumour that the building was to be converted into a commercial warehouse. In a protest group which is large and open and forms a loose-knit social network such rumours are liable to public inspection and are probably rejected or moderated. In a small, tightly knit group they are incorporated into the un-opposed orthodoxy. In these situations the pressure group is set in its ideology of conspiracy or apathy, and the council officials retreat into an overt ideology of legalistic formalism. This is not to say there is necessarily merely a 'breakdown of communications'. Quite the contrary, there may be a conspiracy, there may be genuine and irreducible conflict of interest. In the same way the 'open' type pressure group is not regarded as more rational or more efficacious: its mode of operation simply allows it to take part in a political process according to certain accepted forms.

One of the ways in which the pressure group comes to participate is by bureaucratizing itself. Instead of writing to the council as individuals, the protesters make themselves corporate, write a constitution, elect officers, make claims on their membership. In order to gain credibility and respectability they will probably invite councillors to join and on occasion to become, say, their president. This is felt by some members to give them also a vote in the town hall; others resist such instrusion as 'them' getting their feet under the table. Some councillors are seen as good fellows, others as carpet-baggers. When they are formally constituted the pressure groups call public meetings, to which they invite council officials. They constitute committees or sub-committees to deal with town-hall departments and increasingly learn the town hall's language. Officers of the pressure group, when they have undertaken negotia-tions with the town-hall departmental bureaucracy, will wish to present the result as the best possible outcome in the circumstances. Rank-and-file activists may see this as a sell-out or as a manifestation of the protest group leaders' becoming an agent of the bureaucracy. The leaders may even be drawn into the local authority tendency to secrecy, as we saw in Chapter 6. The process of developing an organizational structure capable of dealing with the council leads to a situation in which the 'leaders' may come to have different interests, especially in the short term, from their 'followers'. This is not to subscribe to an Iron Law or Oligarchy, since the leaders of this sort of pressure group may constitute the 'olig' part but not usually the 'archy'. Members come and go, groups go out of existence because of apathy, new groups may be set up. In a situation of speed, on the other hand, where there is not sufficient time to constitute a formal corporate body, a small close-knit core with organizational resources and expertise is able to take control of a protest to great effect. The notion that the development of bureaucracy over time and the inherent technical complexity of operating a bureaucratic movement inevitably leads to greater control by the officers is clearly not valid. There is a relationship which needs to be examined, but it needs to be looked at in the context of a variety of social resources, of which bureaucratic expertise in a given situation is but one. We shall consider this point below.

Council officials react differently to pressure-group activity in terms of age, ideological prejudices, status, aims, perceptions. Some regard all pressure groups as troublemakers: a public health official may see all who object to compulsory purchase schemes as middle-class suburbanites standing in the way of progress; squatters' movements are written off as the activities of 'students', and reference is made to the huge scale of the housing problem as a reason for not being able to back-pedal in individual cases. A town manager or senior town clerk's department official, however, whose ob involves integrating different departmental views, may see the pressure group as one more standpoint that has to be accounted for, or more cynically perhaps as one more obstacle that has to be skilfully avoided or removed.

There appear to be a number of procedures that have to be gone through in working out a council pressure-group conflict, which involve the availability of different strategies, different needs and different relationships of power for the protesters, government personnel and the press who become involved. At the outset, when a group of individuals decide they are in conflict with some council policy, they must announce this conflict – declare war. Sometimes this may be a matter of *res ipse loquitur* – Manchester Council's plan to build houses on the city's two largest parks only needed to be publicized by the press. The large majority of those who lived around the parks regarded it as self-evident that such a move was antagonistic to their interests. Similarly plans for turning old-established grammar schools into comprehensives can be relied on to call forth salivation, tail-wagging, bristling of neck-hair and barking on the part of Pavlovian parents and old boys/girls. The press formulates such propositions as 'good stories', since the editor and reporter can both forecast a controversial response. For the local authority bureaucracy a head-on collision is expected and they are steeled to the fact that the decision has been taken at the representative democracy level. They are seen, probably accurately, as merely technical functionaries. Politicians are active proponents of policy and the clash between public and council will probably be reflected in a council debate. The leaders of such a protest have to capitalize on the groundswell, and establish their claim to the leadership in a situation where there may be many claimants for the title.

However, most campaigns do not involve such an unambiguous, Pearl Harbor-type inception. In the case of the council's taking action which a local group opposes it is first necessary to establish that the council is taking action. As we have seen, the council official's definition of an action is not a very inclusive one. This constitutes the council's first line of defence: the denial that anything is actually being done. The pressure-group leaders need to persuade potential members that this is not the case and at this point may go to the local press which needs something, such as a public meeting or petition, on which to hang a story – in the absence of a council meeting. Only one of the pressure-group leaders interviewed by the author admitted advocating and using exaggerated rumour as a deliberate means of setting wheels in motion.

Where an actual decision is published by the council, where the council goes so far as to show its proposals to the people involved, as in the Garden Meadows redevelopment scheme, it can still avoid an acknowledgement of direct conflict by insisting that its plans are not finalized, by asserting the notion of departmental autonomy and by retreat into technicism. The planning department claims that it cannot formulate detailed plans until the health committee has actually effected compulsory purchase and clearance orders. Nothing could be decided which would pre-empt such decisions. The health department cannot say anything until the public health officer's report, based on his survey, is complete. The report, it is then insisted, is based purely on the twelve standards of fitness for human habitation laid down in the housing act. The sum of these positions is that nothing can be undertaken in terms of promise or agreement until after a decision is made, and then when the decision is made no agreement can be undertaken which goes beyond the ambit of the decision. Catch 22.

A further stratagem which the council can employ is to accept that it is in conflict with the pressure group but to deny that the conflict is necessarily with a representative proportion of those affected: the troublemaking minority hypothesis. In the Garden Meadows campaign the health department officials questioned the claim that the majority of residents in the clearance actually did oppose the council plans. One of the council officials indeed said that he thought that those who protested against such plans were middle class and not in the actual clearance houses, the occupants of which were only too ready to move into new modern houses. There was indeed truth in the view that the leading lights among the protesters were predominantly middle class, but it was highly questionable that this applied to the rest.

The stratagems available to the pressure-group activists are then to document support, as in the Garden Meadows campaign, by a survey of the clearance area, a referendum of the area, a petition. In the opposition to the scheme to build homes in the parks a mass protest was organized at the town meeting. On other occasions public meetings are mounted, at which councillors and/or officials are subjected to the demonstrable opposition of a hall filled with voters. Councillors and officials are not keen to provide hostages to fortune at such confrontations, and to draw the representatives of protest into the departmental infrastructure provides a more satisfactory alternative. To change a blanket opposition into a detailed argument about what parts of a council proposal are most objectionable alters the nature of the debate qualitatively, since those who are ready to compromise are hived off from the diehards. Each detail in a complex negotiation will show the weaknesses in cohesion where they exist. A hypothetical redevelopment scheme including shops, offices, a new road and threat of kulak treatment for the residents of old property and a clearance order to help commercial landlords empty houses they need for property development will antagonize almost everyone in an area. Those who object lock stock and barrel to change will form a hard core of opposition; although if they are old as is often the case, not a very effective one. But if the rest of the scheme is separated from the new road proposals, those who were mainly objecting on road grounds will be modified. If guarantees are given to rehouse tenants within, say, half a mile of their present homes, many previous opponents will become fervent supporters. If a guarantee of no tower-block development is given, more support for the scheme would likely follow. Socialist ideological opposition will be neutralized by substituting a compulsory purchase order for a clearance order and so attacking the private landlord. Now it obviously depends on the degree of cohesion in the pressure group to what extent movement on the local authority's part will induce a level of quiescence necessary to plough on with a scheme. Sufficient movement may of course be constructed by the protesters as a victory. This may then be referred to by other pressure groups in formulating their own strategies and in making exhortations to their followers. An early and successful campaign by the residents of Crab Lane in north Manchester against a Manchester Corporation redevelopment scheme was constantly referred to by other groups as a sign of the way things must go. Formal contact by letter between pressure leaders may result and may even be followed by joint action where interests seem closely enough allied.

The press has considerable significance for the protesters in these endeavours. Press reports of council meetings are a source of news of expected council action. Press coverage is sought to give notice to those involved that an 'action group' or protection association is being formed. However, issues which involve detailed considerations of departmental bargaining and interdepartmental differences violate a crucial need of all news stories – that of unadorned starkness. The length, the nature of the language, the notion of subbing from the bottom all militate against complexity. Editors in any event want news to be unambiguous – it is a commodity which is quickly consumed. There are alternative sources of communication, as we have seen. Duplicated news-sheets are used to keep members and residents informed. News travels along gossip-networks despite the alleged 'impersonal' nature of the city. It was interesting to note how the so-called 'secondary' associations (usually seen as vast and impersonal by contrast with locality which is seen as a residue of pre-urban 'primary' associations) generate and facilitate inter-locality personal contacts. In the cases studied by the author, inter-personal contact was made at the university, at the airport, at national newspapers and among the council staff at the town hall. Talking to other people is one of the commonest activities in organizations; it is not simply idle chatter, but a mechanism, as it were, of survival. Uncertainty is generated in organizations about how individuals are regarded by other, more powerful individuals, what plans are being made for reorganization, who is leaving and might be replaced by some alarming 'new broom'. In an organization it soon becomes known that Elsie in Maths general office is a Resident's Action Group member, and that Bert in Town Planning had something to do with canals. The secondary super-local level of association may well involve more face-to-face interaction, more gossip, more competition over status, more mate selection (all more characteristically associated with village life) than the dispersed suburb. In the cases we have considered it certainly provided a level of association feeding of information into the localities. It also provided a source whereby people discovered they lived in the same locality.

But although these channels of communication are important in the actual organization of a pressure group when protesters engage in a propaganda war, the press and other news media eclipse all other forms of communication in importance. Indeed at this stage much of what is being done by the pressure group takes on a reality only inasmuch as it is reported in the press. Not only the local authority but the followers in the pressure group are likely to judge the efficacy of, or more precisely to become aware of, the existence of the political agitation of the leaders as a result of press coverage. And in turn other pressure leaders also use press coverage of such activities as a source of ideas for their own armouries. These leaders engage in an ideological game with the council and with the news media. They attempt to depict themselves and reality in accordance with this ideology and they use a number of resources to accomplish this end. At the same time they prospect for the hidden mental states and external constraints of their adversaries: What sort of story will they publish in the *Evening News*? How does the public health department react to petitions, appeals for help, head-on conflict? In this way they use knowledge acquired from a variety of sources, especially from other pressure groups and members who are either 'old campaigners' or those who have inside knowledge.

However, where the pressure is not orientated to long-term activity or to policy change one would not expect the sort of progressive bureaucratization, breakdown of issues into negotiable details and subsumption of leaders into a semi-official limb. There are two sorts of conflict which appeared from the author's research markedly to depart from this tendency. One is the short, sharp 'victorious' campaign. The victory may depend on a number of factors. In the case of the Parkland Action Group they had clear democratic resources in the shape of a town meeting and a town poll which, given sufficient logistic and propaganda skill, they could capitalize on and use to bring a quick defeat of the council proposals. Their organization was geared to this pace. The logistic and propaganda skill could not produce a certain victory at the polls, but it could guarantee the presence of troops at the town meeting; it was a necessary but not a sufficient condition. Internal knowledge of or participation in local government, or personal acquaintance with powerful individuals by members of a pressure group, may on the other hand enable them to engineer a successful outcome to a campaign without either publicity or overt sign of conflict. The difficulty here is in identifying what has happened, especially since the endemic tendency to secrecy in local government means that changes may well be formulated in a form of words of the 'it's-what-we-meant-to-all-along' type. Further, it may not be a policy change which is sought but the rejection of a policy recommendation in an officer's report which has never actually been effected or made public. Such was the case in the threatened closure of an adult education centre: the locals who wished to maintain it had the support of a highly placed officer of the education department who was also able to lobby councillors behind the scenes and the case was settled without an overt acknowledgement of any dispute by the education department.

The second nonconforming instance was the campaign which was centred on the notion that local government was in some way being conducted in bad faith, or that the procedures of local politics themselves were corrupt or potentially corrupt. In these cases the declaration of war is an end in itself and the newspaper's function for the protesters is not that of a passive recipient and processor of information. To report the issue becomes an action in itself, which requires a complex process of inquiry as a preparation. The newspaper or television company has to move into the firing-line. Consensus-orientated 'established' pressure groups and consensus-orientated politicians are unwilling to sponsor such causes and in any event accept that the system and their colleagues do not act in bad faith and are not corrupt. The press for the reasons referred to does not take up the stories. A Mertonian reaction formation appears to be the likely consequence with an apathetic bitterness or cynicism on the part of the campaigners, resulting from a failure to see their perceived grievances attended to by the established political structure, and the almost inevitable collapse of the protest.

Certain social resources or social capital appear to be advantageous or even necessary to achieve recognized participation in the political game. Some of these are specific to situations, but others are general and transferable. Specific resources, such as participation of specific gossip-networks, employment in particular organizations, access to particular rich men are obvious advantages, which are not transferable at the same level of importance. To be more explicit: an officer in one local authority may be able to use his position to obtain papers or to make contact with councillors in the area of his own local authority. In another local authority his advantage would be at a different level: his general knowledge of procedures would indicate what sort of papers might be available, his experience of local government would indicate to him the differences between formal presentation of power relationships and those appertaining in the effective discussion and bargaining about policy at official level. Clearly there are general social resources such as wealth and coercive force which are identified widely, and especially by Marxists,[36] as the means by which the powerful remain powerful. But there are also cognitive resources. As Bernstein[37] and other educational sociologists have shown, mastery of certain linguistic usages, and associated normative views, are associated with economic and social privilege. Clearly the middle class succeed better in general in political affairs than do manual workers. They have 'managerial skills' – or they believe they have them; they often have experience of bureaucratic usages: they are used to writing, telephoning, formulating arguments in reports in a way that manual workers are not. The term middle class includes solicitors, accountants, architects, journalists, who all have skills directly relevant to playing the political games. Middle-class activists know the rules.

But some middle-class activists fail while some working-class activists succeed in gaining access to the political game. The reason for this appears to be ideological. Marxists[38] argue that the bourgeoisie remain economically and politically powerful because of their control over the media, through which in turn they exercise ideological hegemony over the working class. This would seem to postulate the notion that the working class have a 'natural' or 'inevitable' working-class ideology from which they are diverted by an identifiable bourgeois-capitalist, ideological imperialism. Since they reject the notion that Labour reflects this ideology but in fact constitutes a means whereby an essentially capitalist system[39] is maintained, and since the overwhelming bulk of the manual working class are either Labour or Tory supporters, it is hard to see how the conclusion can be drawn that the media do divert the people from their true ideological stance. The evidence, such as it is, is consistent either with the proposition that the system is so successful that the natural proletarian outlook of the working class has been entirely smothered, or that the working class are naturally ideologically committed to the dominant consensus. The operation of the political/ideological game seems not so much to distinguish *directly* against the manual working class in this way but against the ideological nonconformist who might be a 'militant', if a trade unionist, a 'left-wing extremist', if a student, 'irresponsible', if a journalist on an 'underground' journal. In the case of the small local protest this labelling process is made unnecessary by the tacit and, usually, indirect processes of exclusion. Those processes in turn, by reducing to a minimum the expression of overt and explicit objections to the political system, further strengthen an image of a political life relatively untainted by self-interest and producing little discontent among the governed. Ideological conformity – the ability to construct reality and political debates in terms of the dominant rules of political competition – is a resource as important as wealth, prestige, or general educational and managerial skills.

8

Postscript: methods and prescriptions

In this chapter we shall discuss both the methods which I have employed to investigate the nature of the coverage and the non-coverage of local politics in the British press. We shall also discuss what it seems possible to do to improve the parlous state of affairs which various writers have described and attempted to analyse both in Britain and the United States.

My original intention in investigating the local press was to do so by methods generally covered by the ragbag description 'participant observation'. For an undergraduate dissertation I had spent four months working as a reporter on a local weekly newspaper and had noted the events of each day in the normal manner of writing up 'field notes'. Some of my observations were unusable because the nature of events is inevitably specific and involves individuals in periods of stress. Most of the material relating to a close observation of the reporter at work was defective, naturally enough, because it was a case of the reporter observing himself. Moreover it did not seem greatly to add to what I already knew from working as a reporter for five years previously.

My next foray into the field of participant observation was to be more directly an observer and less a participant. In one newspaper this proved relatively successful, except that if you sit in a newspaper office observing the reporters you spend most of the day by yourself answering the telephone, which, though informative in itself, is not sufficient. Also, when you go out with reporters on stories you have to assume the role of a pork-pie at a Jewish wedding. And in that capacity I found that I discovered little more than I knew already, in the sense of having been for many years a 'lay member'. For a more dispassionate analysis it would probably have been better to have stayed away from newspapers altogether, and made my study instead from within a detached analytical framework. Indeed the proprietor of one newspaper certainly shared this view and cast me out of his establishment.

My aim was to study the interaction between newspapermen and their contacts, originally from the point of view of the newspaper as an organization. Because I wanted to look at processes of interaction and organization and not at static pictures of 'attitudes' or at correlations between categories of journalists (e.g. cosmopolitan-local) and categories of newspaper organization (e.g. mechanistic-organismic) I rejected the idea of using a questionnaire survey. In any event such an approach was unsuitable simply because answers to questionnaires are principally not data about people in the context of the area defined by the problem but data about the way people answer questionnaires, and involve forcing on to the actors a model of relevance which is that of sociologist not of the actor.[1] What I was concerned with was the interaction of individuals, which in Weberian terms[2] meant what was subjectively meaningful for them. However, this meant deriving an explanation which was adequate for the data, not finding data adequate to support the explanation. I therefore discovered 'grounded theory'[3] and approached the problem with great confidence, by the well-known process of disproving adequately to myself any alternative to my own position and inferring from this that I was right!

Having discovered that participant observation was a highly defective mode of investigation, because it provided only random pieces of information and because it no more released me from my own construction of reality than would a questionnaire, I also found that the type of observation I had engaged in had produced a picture of something I already knew about: the organization of the local newspaper office, with the activities of the outside world being processed into it as inputs into a Parsonian system. But such a view of an organization was unacceptable to me. I therefore wished to provide myself with data which would enable me to formulate an analysis of the activities of the journalist as part of interrelated processes of interaction and communication among various actors in the local political and social arenas. The difficulty with this exercise was that if the study of newspaper activity began with the newspaper reporter or the newspaper office, any view of the process of communication, interaction, bargaining and negotiation which had preceded the involvement of the paper, would only be available *ex post facto*. The alternative was to seek out a story first and then wait for the newspapers to find it, usually as a result of an approach to the newspaper by the actors involved.

I have indicated earlier what seemed to be the characteristics of a 'good story', but I did not find stories by measuring events against some cogent and intellectually derived criteria. I watched events taking place by joining in local pressure-group activities; I did some plumbing for a housing action group, provided the documents for a television film. Various events seemed to me to coalesce into what I as a reporter would have regarded as a story, or even a good story. Sometimes a local activist would ask how to approach the press and I told him. This did not and does not seem to me to be an impermissible method: I wanted to see what would happen in given circumstances and I was never in a position, nor am I arrogant enough to believe I had the ability, to generate those circumstances. But whenever I could help the process along by technical advice, or even making a billboard to announce a meeting, I did so.

The substantive obstacles that stood between me and the data out of which the stories were to be constructed, were generally those faced by the reporter, but with some differences. In the two cases of councillors and their business deals there were various difficulties in the way of getting hold of the data at all. The first of these was council secrecy. The council epitome of the monthly committee minutes is usually a very sparse document, although it varies from authority to authority. A decision may be indicated which may simply put into effect the recommendations in a town clerk's or an education officer's report, while the report itself is not included in the minutes but remains private and confidential. In this respect I found that I had a considerable advantage over the newspaper reporter. As a research worker from a university I could write to the appropriate authorities and would be allowed to look at the official documents without difficulty. As a reporter I had never enjoyed the facilities thus provided. Equally I could spend hours browsing through minutes looking for clues, whereas the reporter would have a very limited time to do so, supposing that he were given access.

The opening of council committees to the press and public is a matter of very little moment from the point of view of 'opening up' local governmen'. The decisions are not made by committees so much as sub-committees of committees and by party groups, usually resulting from the reports of officers based upon technical expertise, and they often contain complex arguments about the bureaucratic requirement of central government and of local government legislation. These sources remain closed to public scrutiny.

The second problem I was faced with was the complexity of the business involved. In both cases I have simplified the accounts as much as possible while at the same time as making them unidentifiable. A plethora of detail would not only make them immediately recognizable to those concerned, but incomprehensible to everyone else. For the reporter this approach would present a considerable problem because he has to work to a deadline and cannot go back repeatedly to check on details, whereas for the sociologist the time-scale does not generate the same degree of pressure. It is important of course to get the facts reasonably straight before the actors die, move away or forget all about them.

The sources of information against which one can check all have to be used in order to build up a picture that represents a common reality, and what should therefore be free of the taint of defamation. Let me explain this by reference to the way in which I would proceed through a variety of sources and build up data about a 'story'. At the same time what would also emerge would be a picture of the social relationship between the actors involved and, as they sent me along the networks, a picture of the more significant links in the network for them in relation to the passage of this information. My picture of these links was not formulated on the basis of the sort of general question devoid of content, such as about whom did they interact with most, but on specific ones of this type: Who told you about X? Or, whom did you tell about X? Or, how will I find out more about X? Or, who else do you think knows about X? In other words I judged the strength of the network in terms of the practical day-to-day use it was put to or seen as being put to by the members.

The first source I found essential was, needless to say, the informant. Now in the case of the newspaper this would be a contact either providing a tip-off or attempting to get coverage for a grievance, a regular contact or possibly the corporate person of the local authority speaking with the voice of the monthly minutes or publicity handouts. I did not of course have regular informants, although a number of people did come to me with tales of dark deeds. My main source at this level were the speakers at meetings at which I was 'a participant observer'. When someone made an allegation that a developer or a politician was up to something, or that a group of squatters had taken over a street, I would go and check with them afterwards. Now the reporter under constant pressure to produce copy as a result of his efforts would not have the luxury of being able to wander around and talk to anybody who took his fancy in the hope that one might produce a good story. Frequently the first person in the chain, once contacted, proves to be of little use. One such informant, a woman, told me about a plot which involved a group of councillors all buying land and selling it to one another, in which endeavour they were assisted by most of the staff of the local authority. Apart from the fact that the conspiracy seemed a trifle all-inclusive it was not supported by much evidence other than a general fear that her house was next on the list. However, about a year later I heard another member of the same pressure group referring to the same set of events, although this was not apparent until I had interviewed him later for several hours, because his claims were specific, restricted and related to documented evidence. Another informant told me of a man waging war against a local authority which he claimed, had deprived him of his rightful promotion and pension as a result of his having attempted to rectify certain corrupt practices in the department in which he had worked as an official. He had attempted to get redress by the press and through his Member of Parliament. His aim was a ministerial inquiry. He claimed to have papers which proved his case, but the large pile of documents he produced did not support his contention. It is true they showed that what he said related to real events, in the sense that contracts were referred to and costings were given. (In the margins he had written such comments as 'all lies!') And there were various documents from high-ranking council officials to other high-ranking officials referring to the man's case which he had surreptitiously 'found' in their filing cabinets and photocopied. They referred to him as being ill and generally hinted that he was of unsound mind, and their general tone was hysterical and paranoid. This is quite a normal reaction by those in authority when challenged but it could only 'prove' they were persecuting the man if one accepted that his accusations of fraud which related to a period just after the Festival of Britain were true.

I checked the story with the first of the witnesses the informant had mentioned, and I was prepared to trek the country in pursuit of numerous local authority officials who had been in the offending department when the irregularities had allegedly occurred nearly twenty years before. The first witness was a senior official in a local authority elsewhere in the country. He was head of his department and had reasonable expectation of being made head of it in a reconstituted authority, of which his present one was to form the largest component element. Whereas my informant, the victim, was small and old and broken, this official was a large successful, well-paid man with a powerful handshake. Yes, everything my informant had said was true. The authority had been a den of thieves. Officials had been taking backhanders from contractors. They had been tipping off certain firms about competitor's prices. The favoured firms then tendered low prices and won contracts, later increasing their prices to more than those of their competitors while the work was in progress. This they were able to do by invoking an increased costs clause which should only have been used to take account of price rises for raw materials or labour or maintenance after the commencement of the contract. The original tenders were, said this witness, inadequately formulated from the point of view of bills of quantities, so that the local authority was buying a pig in a poke, which they paid for later through the increased costs clause.

Yes, it was true that condemned materials marked as such by honest quantity surveyors with the department were then moved to new sites by building contractors where other quantity surveyors would turn a blind eye. Yes, one day he had seen with my informant perished cement with a blue mark on the bags, indicating it had been previously condemned, being used by a council contractor. Yes, it was true that when together they had raised this aberration with their departmental chief he had threatened them and told them to keep quiet. My informant was then moved to another department because of his non-professional behaviour towards contractors. For his part my present witness has been threatened with physical ejection by the head of the department but he brandished his fist and as a result, it seems, was given good references and left.

The successful man now contacted his ex-colleague, the victim, to see how he was. He was rather distressed to think of his old friend being brought so low by a combination of events and his own incapacity to deal with them. The victim then telephoned me to say that both he and his wife were ill and that they were being given tranquillizers. If I did not drop my inquiries he could not be responsible for what happened. He rang me several more times saying that he felt on the verge of suicide. Not only did I have to drop the case, but I had to visit him several times to reassure him that I had done so. This meant calling when his wife was not there in order not to upset her.

The difficulty in dealing with an organizationally defined deviant is that he is balked all the time by the fact that his story and his deviant label are inextricably intertwined. If a member of an organization is being treated as a paranoiac, this provides him with the evidence that he is being persecuted, but the result is that what he says is construed by listeners as being the product of his paranoid fantasies, with the result that these listeners unwittingly enlist themselves in the conspiracy against him. So long as he is believed to be paranoid, almost anything he says or does can be ascribed to his fantasies; while all the responses by the organizationally defined 'normal' can be interpreted by him as further proof of the existence of an inclusive plot against him.

In assessing the stories related by informants, I came to the conclusion that organizations which are characterized by secrecy and power, i.e. bureaucracies, are of their nature conducive to paranoid reactions by members. In the absence of knowledge about the grounds on which decisions are made, subordinates are likely to interpret decisions which adversely affect their interests as being undertaken specifically to damage their interests. In turn, their strategies to protect their own interests are interpreted by superordinate officials as conspiratorial rebellions. One of the protest groups I observed was in conflict with a local authority department over a plan to close down a public building, though one official in the department wanted the building to be kept open. The fight between the two officials concerned had gone on over a number of years. Both men were in positions a little below chief officer level, one being slightly senior to the other. One bone of contention was the fact a departmental prospectus had been brought out with the junior man relegated to a position not usually occupied by an officer of his standing. Now, he told me, he did not mind this: what concerned him was why it had been done and what motives his senior had had. He told me of a confidential report by the senior man which suggested that the junior was not carrying out the duties officially assigned to him. When I found the report in the bowels of the town hall it did seem to say as much. It also implied that the junior officer was unwilling to carry out the instructions of the senior: which was true. When I interviewed a close assistant of the senior official he told me that they all knew what the junior man was up to: 'He's an empire builder. He's just using the issue as a means for furthering his own power.' When eventually the matter came before a committee meeting of councillors, the junior official lobbied politicians of both parties for support and won his case.

The relationship between officials who are in a state of conflict or competition is rather like that of two super-powers in an arms' race. Neither knows what the other is doing, so he invents a 'scenario' to explain his opponent's behaviour, and conducts his strategies in order to thwart the hypothesized strategies of his opponent. His own behaviour then confirms, if needs be, a conspiracy hypothesis on the part of his opponent, who in turn behaves in a way which confirms the other's conspiracy scenario. This is not to say that conflicts are in truth bred by distrust and paranoid fantasy. It is just as legitimate to interpret the distrust as the outcome of genuine conflicts of interest, and the behaviour although paranoid in appearance as not simply paranoid, because the actors actually are plotting against one another.

The pursuit of truth through the neighbourhood or the protest group is less hazardous. In the Marlborough Drive case study I was sent from one neighbour to another clarifying details and returning to check until I had built up a clear picture of what deals had taken place and what council decisions had been made. For instance, I wanted to compare the date of the actual purchase of the land with the granting of planning permission and the change of the planning restriction. I asked Mr Braine, who thought that the land was bought before the planning blight was lifted, which meant that Simon's brother would have had an interest in the land at the time the council voted on the issue and that the town clerk's report to the redevelopment sub-committee must have been inaccurate. But he was not sure of this. He suggested I should see Mrs Duddon, since it was she who had told him about the planning side of the affair. Mrs Duddon was certain that Simon owned the land when the council lifted the planning restriction, but she did not know the exact date. She said she was sure that Mr Thorne would tell me, since he now regretted having sold the land to Simon. Accordingly I approached Thorn and he gave me the exact date and price, which confirmed that the land was in Simon's possession both at the time the council lifted the ban and when it granted the planning persmission. However, contracts had not been exchanged at the time of the redevelopment sub-committee meeting, although the negotiations were complete and the documents were ready for signature. The fact that signatures were only put to the documents after the sub-committee made its decision was interpreted by the Marlborough Drive group as evidence that Simon was using information he had acquired about confidential sub-committee resolutions before these decisions were ratified or made public. It also meant that the town clerk's report although not at fault for not referring to Simon's ownership, as that had not materialized until after the sub-committee meeting, was out of date both at the full General Purposes Committee meeting and at the council. Furthermore, it could not have noted that a councillor and a councillor's relative had an interest in the outcome of the council's deliberations on the question. In order to clarify the situation further, I procured photocopies of the documentation of various aspects of the sale and of the council decisions.

In this instance then there were several 'facts', in the sense that they were recorded in bureaucratically legitimated records, which I was able to establish by working through a gossip-network. This also rendered data about the gossip-network and about how the members perceived the 'facts' which I was seeking. I was then able to seek among official papers for information I wanted. The official documents had relevance for me because I was looking for proof or disproof of what I had been told. It would have been virtually impossible to get at the data otherwise, because much of its details of land transactions are hidden in solicitors' files or in the land registry where they can only be seen either by an owner or by someone with an interest in the land – a prospective purchaser who has first had the owner's permission, for instance.

Official documents do provide a rich seam of information about the processes of local government and about business interests of councillors, provided the searcher knows what he is looking for. The registrar of Friendly Societies keeps records of housing associations, for example. These include the names of the management committee, the value of assets and expenses. Several such associations operating from one address may well have the same members on the management committee. Where one of these members owns the premises, which may be a building firm or an estate agent's office or both, it is possible to check through the Registry of Companies at Company House in London for the names and interests of those involved, and these firms may of course have as a result a financial stake in such housing associations. It may be that if all the housing associations have a common 'management agent' one can add up the estate management fees and check the figures against the annual takings of a registered estate management company, and also check the income of the directors.

Not all businesses are registered in this way, and so they are not open to scrutiny. Equally, returns to the Registrar of Friendly Societies are not always very informative. If one is looking for the figure paid for a particular plot of land it is not likely to be recorded, and other transactions may be covered by the formula 'cash analysis not readily available'. Again one man may be a director of several different businesses. Other businesses may operate in the name of relatives from other addresses. These companies may lend money to one another and purchase land from one another.

The actual interviewing of officials and politicians presents different difficulties respectively for the reporter and the academic research worker. The reporter announces himself as the representative of a newspaper and has a reason for being seen and asking specific questions. Unless, that is, he has the misfortune to work for a small and newly founded local weekly (as I did), when the following sort of conversation often takes place:

'Hello, is that the town clerk? It's the *Gazette* here.'

'Yes, Williams speaking. The who?'

'The *Gazette*. The local newspaper.'

'Oh yes, the *City Press*. You're the ones who publish from Southport. You got my name wrong last week.'

'No, the *Gazette*. We publish from Preston. It was the *City Press* which got your name wrong last week.'

'Yes, I know. The name's Williams, *not* Williamson. Funny though I was sure you published from Southport. Your paper's always full of Southport advertisements and stories.'

'No, that's the *City Press*. We're the *Gazette*. We publish from Preston. If anything, we have a lot of Preston ads in our paper.'

'There seems to be a misunderstanding. This council doesn't have anything to do with Southport – I mean Preston.'

'Nor do we. . . .'

Provided the newspaper is either a well-known national or an establishment local institution the reporter is thought to have a normal everyday purpose in approaching officials for a story. Generally, local officials do not want to antagonize or perhaps more appropriately frighten newspaper reporters, since they have the means to provide favourable publicity for the local authority. But when the official sees the reporter he is less likely to give him background information about events and less likely to pass on information about intra-departmental antagonisms, for fear of the effect of publicity.

The research associate or Ph.D. student for his part has a difficult time trying to obtain interviews with a specific individual. Normally a sociologist undertakes a study of a situation where he is accepted, having made previously a number of approaches, many of which will have been turned down. When he is pursuing a tale, however, there is another discipline, since a particular official or councillor will be required to give certain pieces of information or rebut given allegations. I found that when I did gain access as an academic, officials, contacts and politicians were more forthcoming than had been the case when I was journalist, but on the other hand approaches were more often ignored or appointments not kept. One councillor arranged to see me on a day he was in France. Perhaps a professorial handle would provide greater purchase.

Finally, perhaps the greatest difficulty is in negotiating a role in such a situation. In my case reactions varied from irritation at my presence to ones in which I was regarded as a 'professional' who could carry out inquiries more satisfactorily than amateur members of a pressure group. The latter, although more flattering to my vanity, was rarer than the former by a factor of at least several hundred per cent. In the event of simply watching events it was easiest to find something which I could actually do: in this respect making billboards and sandwich-boards or undertaking a repair to the plumbing of a house occupied by squatters was more valuable than acting out the role of a group confessor or any other suspect intellectual role. Equally, the provision of concrete information or a file of documents or arranging an interview with an informant gave me a role at the television company, whereas I do not think that the activists or I would have been comfortable if I had merely sat in the office making notes in the interest of western culture and my Ph.D. thesis.

If the relationship between the observer and the observed in a given situation is difficult, moving from one situation to another is even more difficult. To be a supporter of a group of squatters one day and a detached observer in the company of a town-hall official the next puts one in a two-faced category, broadly that of a liar. On one occasion an informant gave me a piece of information in the expectation that I would provide him with documents which a third person had apparently stolen. The third party only agreed to give me the papers if I promised not on any account to give them to the first person. I wrestled briefly with my conscience and won by a submission in the first round. I decided to compromise and kept the documents myself, making photocopies for the first person. In that way I had been strictly fair and at the same time equally dishonest with all concerned, while attempting to provide a degree of compliance which they would find acceptable.

In writing about the sort of the cases I studied, the newspaper reporter can only resort to the course of action I have indicated: he can leave it out, far and away the most common solution; or he can write it up in generalized, consensus-supporting terms; or risk libel by pushing his work to the extreme of what is acceptable in terms of the consensus. The sociologist, on the other hand, can opt for what I have done here, under the compulsion of counsel's advice, and alter the names, places and events sufficiently so that they cannot be regarded as libellous, because no one is actually identifiable. The reasons for this being unsatisfactory hardly need to be enumerated. Plainly, I am dealing in documentary fiction, and the reader has to take my word for it that I have gone to great trouble to produce replicas of the real cases, the real cases having been documented by me in great detail as a result of months of work in each instance.

Prescriptions

It would be idle to pretend that I find the position of the newspaper in the local political process to be satisfactory, or that the present organization of the local press generates the sort of freedom of expression and exchange of ideas which are claimed for it. The problem of how to arrive at a more satisfactory solution is, however, not easily solved. The release of the paper from the sort of commercialism that leads to the production of a readily saleable bromide which is proof against the backlash of the powerful is not a consummation which can be readily achieved, however devoutly wished. In general, it seems unlikely that a publicly owned press would achieve that end, because it would be dependent on funds and support from the very bureacuracy and politicians whose activities it would in part be intended to scrutinize; and whenever there were periods of financial crisis, insecurity would lead to the sort of bromide which would make national servicemen's tea look like Spanish Dry Fly, to coin a *Daily Mirror*ism.

There does appear to be a solution available, however, in the form of an 'underground press', rather like a network of local *Private Eyes*. These organs are run usually by voluntary labour and rely on a cheap technology. Typing errors and crude reproduction of pictures are accepted as part and parcel of the ventures, as are incredibly long articles on the struggle against fascism in Chile. They are also likely to contain information about protest groups, tales of town-hall barneys and items about the business interests of council members. Where these are inaccurate, the councillors have what seems to me more than adequate means at their disposal to disabuse the public or to take on the papers in the courts. The treatment of some planning stories in these papers is very full, very detailed and accurate. In Manchester the *Manchester Free Press* was started by professional journalists during a printers' strike and maintains a high standard of professionalism. In a number of cases, journalists with stories that their editors turned down for publication in the established commercial press, placed them in the 'Freep' – once at least to the acute embarrassment of the officials in a town-hall department.

A further solution would be to 'open up' the town halls, although I do not believe this to be a simple matter. At present both press and pressure groups are excluded from decisions until it is too late to do anything about them. Typically, pressure groups seeking information *before* a decision is taken are told that nothing has been decided, although officers may have been working on a scheme and have proposals drawn up, while *after* the council has taken a decision it is too late to act. Only in the period between a committee decision and the council's ratification of decisions, a period of probably a fortnight or less, is there the possibility of action.

It might be more satisfactory if, in addition to the present provision for objections through public inquiries with the council's absurdly worded notices in small type glued to lampposts, announcing schemes for redevelopment and the laying down of motorways and other transport schemes, there were public debate and negotiation. It might also help if public participation meant just that and not a public relations exercise to obtain public acceptance of municipal directives. The two areas which most need opening up in this respect seem to me to be planning and the granting of contracts: planning because this is one area of council activity where it is possible to make decisions which radically alter the value of land owned by individuals while at the same time altering the whole character of a town centre. A town centre precinct scheme is likely to be the subject of great publicity and perhaps controversy. But individual plans to redevelop small sites as blocks of flats or as offices go by without great publicity. An individual landowner may obtain a number of adjacent sites and thus acquire a parcel of land with planning permission for redevelopment for each component piece, which can then generate the redevelopment of an area and the commencement of the alteration of a neighbourhood without the consultation of the residents simply, by virtue of the rights of ownership. More important, the decisions by which areas are zoned for industrial or residential development or as green-belt ones should be opened up for public participation. These decisions, which lay ground rules for the future planning decisions on individual sites within a zone, pre-empt future choices in a way which most residents of an area do not understand. In this sort of situation a councillor who is a landowner, or an estate agent or builder, or a property speculator, or a combination of all three, plainly has much to gain from certain decisions. It is hard to divine the logic which prevents the schoolteacher who is an employee of a local authority from being a member while admitting the businessman with a direct interest in the general direction of policy and the carrying out of specific details. The compulsory declaration of an interest at present is not backed by sanctions which are likely to constitute a deterrent, but merely by fines which at most are likely to amount to a mere fraction of the profit to be had in such cases, and then only if the case is brought within a given time period. A compulsory register of councillors' interests would also seem to be required as a minimum, although it must be borne in mind that whatever is done by public compulsion will not prevent behind-the-scenes deals which get round the law without breaking it.

The law of libel presents enormous difficulties, since one is faced with the need primarily to protect private individuals from public attack. It seems to me that a law which protects politicians from any allegation of sharp motives, because such an accusation might cause ridicule and contempt, is mealy-mouthed. This appears to be a perfectly reasonable accusation to make in circumstances where such motives could lead subsequently to action being taken by a politician, especially where such action would reasonably be open to question. More important, where public interest is involved and where facts of a case are proven, it would be helpful if the need to prove innuendo were utterly stringent and known to be so.

The United States is often cited as a model towards which the British press might aspire, because of its independence and investigative zeal. Moreover, the enshrinement of the 'fourth estate' in the constitution is seen as providing the newspaperman with a security in his search for information not enjoyed by the British journalist, who is in a grace-and-favour situation in relation to politicians and official sources of news. At the same time the American political system is much more open in the sense that the constitutional arrangements between the different arms of government lead to a constant public examination of executive policies.

The evidence about the effect of the American press at the local level does not fill one with confidence about its operation, however. For instance, the study by Paletz and his associates of a local paper in Cleveland suggest that the local newspaper supports the local community élite by its reconstruction of events in the town council, which are often chaotic and disordered, into an apparently rationalized and purposeful set of activities.[4] Janowitz's study of three Chicago local newspapers suggests that the local press is concerned to promote 'community enhancing' stories, and that where a government agency is the subject of criticism or a conflict-oriented story it is likely to be a government agency not of the locality, e.g. a federal agency. In any case the attack is more than likely to be one which emanates from local politicians, and the local press is seen once again as supporting the local power structure.[5] Robert Park[6]

and Louis Wirth[7] see the American press and especially the immigrant press as the means by which people are integrated into an
existing order: it is a conservative and functional element in the life
of the city. The pre-war community power studies similarly indicate
the existence of local power structures in some American cities and
towns which would have fitted the conspiracy models of the most
hard-line Marlborough Drive activists. Although there are grounds
for rejecting much of the general inferences drawn from the data
of these studies, they do raise questions about the Madisonian
version of American democracy which underlies some of the confidence with which British commentators regard the openness of
the American press and government. Studies of the actual organization of American newspapers themselves suggest also that in many
cases proprietorial control is strong;[8] that choice of news is often
based on the prejudice of certain editorial personnel, or on the pressure of bureaucratic needs of the newspaper organization. Others
suggest that in the news-gathering process certain local gatekeepers
in the supply of news to local newspapers are in a position to exert
crucial influence over news supply.

On the whole then, there is evidence to suggest that the American
system of government the position of the American press and the
American defamation laws appear to favour the journalist and the
newspaper vis-à-vis government by comparison with the position
in Britain: and certainly any move to restrict the endemic, chronic
and pervasive secrecy of government in Britain, and especially of
local government, would be an improvement. But there is no reason
to believe that this would produce more than a marginal improvement, because the constraints on press freedom appear to be in the
nature of the relationship between the press and government and
to stem from the bureaucratic and commercial demands of the
newspaper business. In the context of increasing economic stringency and a contraction in the newspaper jobs anyone who values
the idea of a robust press able to generate a variety of ideas and
provide an informed coverage of political events would have good
grounds for pessimism.

Notes and references

Chapter 1   Introduction

1. For a description of a similar process in the United States see David
L. Paletz, Peggy Reichert and Barbara McIntyre, 'How the Media Support
Local Government Authority', *Public Opinion Quarterly*, Vol. XXXV, 1,
Spring 1971, pp. 80–94.
2. Professor Leslie Derry, a metallurgist undertaking an investigation
into a motorist's death in an accident for a Cambridge inquest in January
1966, suggested that the transverse engined BMC Minis' and 1100s' universal joints transmitting both drive and steering to the front wheels might be
prone to metal fatigue leading to steering failure. Further inquiries
eventually led to the conclusion that this was not the case and the joints
were exonerated from having any role in causing the motorist's death. But
between Derry's initial suggestion at the inquest and the eventual abandon-
ment of the theory, any case of a death or accident involving a transverse
BMC lurching across the road was a saleable commodity. I covered an
inquest for my own very local paper, with a circulation of less than 10,000
at that time, on a man whose car had veered across the road inexplicably.
Because it was a Mini our paper used it as a front-page lead. Because it was
a Mini the press bench, which normally accommodated one reporter
from our paper, a junior from the local freelance agency and another
from the competing weekly, was packed with the massed ranks of hard-
faced national newspaper reporters and freelances who then packed into
an ante-room where they compared shorthand notes, arrived at an author-
ized version of the bits which some had not heard clearly, checked the
spellings of the names with the locals and fled for their cars and telephones.

Chapter 2   The silent watchdog

1. Report of the Royal Commission on the Press, 1947–1949, Cmnd
7700, 1949, Survey by the British Guild of Newspaper Editors, submitted
in evidence.
2. Ministry of Housing and Local Government Commission, The
Management of Local Government, report of the committee, chairman
Sir John Maud (London: HMSO) 1965.
3. *Benn's Newspaper Press Directory* (London: Benn), published annually.
4. Maud, op. cit. (note 2 above).
5. Ominous Empire, unpublished paper by D. S. Morris and K. Newton,
Birmingham University, 1971.
6. A. J. Beith, *The Press and English Local Authorities*, unpublished
B.Litt. thesis, Nuffield College, Oxford, 1968.
7. Beith's figures again provide substantial support for this view as

does Frank Smallwood, in *Greater London, The Politics of Reform* (New York: Bobbs Merrill) 1965, p. 165. Smallwood relates the impoverished coverage of major local government issues in London to the commercialism of chain weeklies but does not develop this theme.

8.   Morris Janowitz, *The Community Press in an Urban Setting* (Chicago University Press) 1967.

9.   Paletz *et al.*, 'How the Media Support Local Government Authority', op. cit.

10.   Janowitz, op. cit., p. 1.

11.   London: Penguin 1970.

12.   *Report of the Royal Commission on the Press 1947–1949*, Cmnd 7700 1949; *Report of the Royal Commission on the Press 1961*, Cmnd 1811–19 (1961). A third royal commission is now sitting.

13.   Hill, op. cit., p. 116.

14.   Ibid., p. 120.

15.   Ibid., p. 131.

Chapter 3   Pluralism and protest groups

1.   Robert A. Dahl, *Who Governs?* (New Haven Conn: Yale University Press) 1961.

2.   Joseph A. Schumpeter, *Capitalism, Socialism and Democracy* (New York: Harper) 1942.

3.   N. Polsby, *Community Power and Political Theory* (New Haven, Conn: Yale University Press) 1963.

4.   Samuel E. Finer, *Anonymous Empire: A Study of the Lobby in Great Britain* (London: Pall Mall) 1958.

5.   Ibid., pp. 94–101.

6.   Ibid., pp. 123–4.

7.   A. J. M. Sykes I. R. Illersic, et al.: 'The Communist Connection', *The Observer*, 3 Feb 1974. This article with academic titles attached to the authors' names was heralded as the report of the Institute for the Study of Conflict on Sources of Conflict in British Industry. It included a table of leading trade unions, showing the balance of power in them and the political complexion of their leaders. Jack Jones of the Transport and General Workers' Union was labelled 'far left'. Mr Jones has subsequently been a leading advocate of the social contract, voluntary wage restraint, and was the originator of the flat-wage increase proposal which has now been accepted by the government.

8.   Clark Kerr and Abraham Siegel, 'Inter-Industry Propensity to Strike', in *Industrial Conflict*, ed. A. Kornhauser, Robert Dubin and Arthur M. Ross (New York: McGraw-Hill) 1954.

9.   Manchester: Manchester University Press 1968.

10.   David Manning White, 'The Gatekeeper: A Case Study in the Selection of News', *Journalism Quarterly* 27 (4) 1950, pp. 383–900. For other references see Chapter 7, notes 10 and 11 below.

11.   The notion of functional deviance suggested in Emile Durkheim, *Rules of Sociological Method* (New York: Free Press) 1964, p. 67.

12.   See Leon Festinger, 'A Theory of Cognitive Dissonance', (London: Tavistock Publications) 1962.

Chapter 4   *Respectable protest*

1. A. V. Cicourel, *Method and Measurement in the Social Sciences* (New York: Free Press) 1964, B. Glazer and A. Strauss (eds.), *The Discovery of Grounded Theory* (London: Weidenfeld and Nicolson) 1967.
2. R. K. Merton, *Social Theory and Social Structure* (New York: Free Press) 1957, pp. 149–55.
3. See R. W. Bacon and W. A. Eltis, 'A Budget Message for Mr Healey: Get More People into Factories', *Sunday Times*, 10 Nov. 1974. The authors are economists.
4. See for instance T. Burns and G. Stalker, *The Management of Innovation* (London: Tavistock) 1971, pp. 77–125; M. Rose, *Computers, Managers and Society* (London: Penguin) 1969, pp. 129–211; E. Mumford, 'Planning for Computers' in *Management Information Systems*, ed. T. W. McRae (London: Penguin) 1971, pp. 317–30.
5. See for instance Peter G. Richards, *The New Local Government System* (London: Allen and Unwin) 1970, and William A. Robson, *Local Government in Crisis* (London: Allen and Unwin) 1966, and others.
6. See A. Dexter and D. M. White (eds.), *People, Society and Mass Communication* (New York: Free Press) 1964, for articles by White, Pool and Gieber.

Chapter 6   *The* Blackville Examiner

1. H. H. Gerth and C. Wright Mills (eds.), *From Max Weber* (London: Routledge & Kegan Paul) 1948, p. 196.
2. Ibid., p. 197.
3. Ibid.
4. Ibid.
5. Ibid.
6. Ibid.
7. Such an inference could be drawn from Emile Durkheim's analysis of the relationship between mechanical solidarity and simple social structures and of the societal breakdown associated with a pathological division of labour – see the *Division of Labour in Society* (New York: Free Press) 1964, pp. 139–377; and from similar arguments in Elton Mayo's *The Social Problems of an Industrial Civilization* (Cambridge, Mass.: Harvard University Press) 1945.
8. R. Goldthorpe and D. Lockwood, *The Affluent Worker: Industrial Attitudes and Behaviour* (Cambridge: Cambridge University Press) 1968, pp. 39–40.

Chapter 7   *Conclusions*

1. There is specific analysis of communication at a microscopic level in such works as Murray Beauchamp's *Elements of Mathematical Sociology* (New York: Random House) 1970, chap. 1, and some of the implications for organization in D. Katz and R. L. Kahn, *The Social Psychology of Organizations* (New York: John Wiley) 1967, pp. 223–58, where the

relationships between individuals in terms of hierarchy and communication are analysed in terms of matrix algebra. In works such as Richard Hyman's *Strikes* (London: Penguin) 1972, or Ralph Miliband's *The State in Capitalist Society* (London: Quartet) 1973, pp. 197–214, the macroscopic relationship between control of communication processes and political power is assumed but not examined analytically.

2.   J. C. Mitchell (ed.), *Social Networks in Urban Situations* (Manchester: Manchester University Press) 1969. The first two chapters are by Mitchell.

3.   K. W. Deutsch, *Nationalism and Social Communication* (Cambridge Technological Press of M.I.T. Mass.) 1953; *The Nerves of Government* (New York: Free Press) 1963.

4.   I. Neustadt, *Presidential Power: The Politics of Leadership* (New York: John Wiley) 1961.

5.   Basil Bernstein, *Class Codes and Control* (London: Routledge & Kegan Paul) 1972.

6.   See Harold Garfinkel, *Studies in Ethnomethodology* (Englewood Cliffs N.J.: Prentice-Hall) 1968, for analyses of the possession of knowledge as a source of social competence, especially the section of Agnes and Wes Sharrock's, 'On Owning Knowledge' in *Ethnomethodology*, ed. Roy Turner (London: Penguin) 1974, pp. 45–53, and numerous others.

7.   Erving Goffman, 'On Facework' in *Interaction Ritual* (Chicago: Aldine) 1967, pp. 5–46.

8.   Peter McHugh, *Defining The Situation* (New York: Bobbs Merrill) 1968, pp. 14–17.

9.   See Warren Breed, 'Social Control in the Newsroom', *Social Forces*, No. 33, 1955, pp. 326–35.

10.   For instance R. E. Carter (Jr), 'Newspaper Gatekeepers and the Sources of News, *Public Opinion Quarterly*, 22 (2), 1958, pp. 133–44, or Lewis Donohew, 'Newspaper Gatekeepers and Forces in the News Channel', *Public Opinion Quarterly*, 31 (1), 1967, pp. 61–9.

11.   On this there are many studies, such as D. Manning White's 'The Gatekeeper: A Case Study in the Selection of News', *Journalism Quarterly*, 27 (4), 1950, pp. 383–90; Walter Gieber, 'Across the Desk: A Study of 16 Telegraph Editors', *Journalism Quarterly*, 33, 1956, pp. 423–32; and also articles by Gieber and White in *People, Society and Mass Communication*, ed., L. A. Dexter and D. M. White (New York: Free Press) 1964.

12.   V. O. Keys' *Public Opinion and American Democracy* (New York: Knopf) 1961, is probably the classic in this tradition. There are numerous such studies reported in the pages of *Public Opinion Quarterly* and *Journalism Quarterly*, e.g. L. Berkowitz's 'Film Violence and Subsequent Aggressive Tendencies', *Public Opinion Quarterly*, 27 (3) 1963, pp. 217–29. Similar studies are scattered elsewhere: see B. Wilson 'Mass Media and the Public Attitude to Crime'. *Criminal Law Review* June 1961, pp. 376–84. For a full bibliography and accounts of the early 'effects' approach to mass communication see Wilbur Schramm (ed.), *The Process and Effects of Mass Communication* (Urbana: University of Illinois Press) 1954, especially Schramm's own article. Also W. Phillips Davison, 'On the Effects of Communication' in *People, Society and Mass Communication*, pp. 68–89.

13. Breed, op. cit., pp. 327–8.
14. Donohew, op. cit.
15. Carter, op. cit.
16. White, op. cit.
17. Gieber, op. cit.
18. Breed, op. cit., pp. 327–8.
19. White, op. cit.
20. Mitchell, op. cit.
21. Janowitz, op. cit.
22. Norton E. Long, 'The Local Community as an Ecology of Games', *American Journal of Sociology*, Vol. 64, Nov. 1958.
23. Op. cit.
24. McHugh, op. cit.
25. E. Bittner, 'The Concept of Organisation' in *Ethnomethodology*, ed. R. Turner.
26. D. H. Zimmerman, 'Record-keeping and the Intake Process in a Public Welfare Organization', in *On Record: Files and Dossiers in American Life*, ed. S. Wheeler, New York: (Russell Sage Foundation) 1969.
27. A. V. Cicourel, *The Social Organization of Juvenile Justice* (New York: Wiley) 1968.
28. H. Molotch and M. Lester, 'News as Purposive Behavior', *American Sociological Review*, Vol. 39, No. 1, 1974, pp. 101–12.
29. G. Tuchman, 'Making News by Doing Work: Routinizing the Unexpected', *American Journal of Sociology*, Vol. 79, No. 1, 1973, pp. 110–31.
30. L. Sigelman, 'Reporting the News: An Organizational Analysis', *American Journal of Sociology*, Vol. 79, 1973, pp. 132–51.
31. See Floyd Hunter, *Community Power Structure* (Chapel Hill: University of North Carolina Press) 1963; Robert S. and Helen M. Lynd, *Middletown in Transition* (New York: Harcourt Brace) 1957; D. C. Miller, 'Decision Making Cliques in Community Power Structure', *American Journal of Sociology*, LXIV, Nov. 1958, pp. 299–310; W. Lloyd Warner and Paul S. Lunt, *The Social Life of a Modern Community* (New Haven, Conn.: Yale University Press) 1941; E. Digby Baltzell, 'Who's Who in America' and 'The Social Register' in *Class, Status and Power*, ed. R. Bendix and S. M. Lipset (London: Routledge & Kegan Paul) 1966, pp. 266–74.
32. For instance R. A. Dahl, *Who Governs?*; N. Polsby, *Community Power and Political Theory*; A. Wildavsky, *Leadership in a Small Town*, Totowa, N.J.: 1964; William Spinrad, 'Power in Local Communities', *Social Problems*, Vol. 12, Winter 1965, pp. 335–56; and Bendix and Lipset, op. cit., pp. 218–30.
33. See the efforts of Robert Dahl in *Modern Political Analysis*, pp. 39–54, and *Who Governs?* respectively to enunciate and put into effect this methodology.
34. Paletz, *et al.*, op. cit.
35. Op. cit.
36. See for instance Robin Blackburn, 'The Unequal Society', in *The Incompatibles*, ed. R. Blackburn and A. Cockburn (London: Penguin) 1967, and Miliband, op. cit., chap. 9 and elsewhere.

37. Bernstein, op. cit.
38. Miliband, op. cit., pp. 197–212.
39. Ibid., pp. 96–102, 182–3; and Andrew Glyn and Bob Sutcliffe, *British Capitalism: Workers and The Profits Squeeze* (London: Penguin) 1972, chap. 8.

Chapter 8   Postscript: methods and prescriptions

1. Cicourel, *Method and Measurement in the Social Sciences*.
2. Weber, *Economy and Society*, ed. G. Roth and C. Wittich (Totowa N.J.: Bedminster) 1968, p. 28. See Wildavsky, p. 254.
3. Glazer and Strauss, *The Discovery of Grounded Theory*.
4. Paletz, *et al.*, 'How the Media Support Local Government Authority', op. cit.
5. Janowitz, *The Community Press in an Urban Setting*.
6. Robert E. Park, *The Immigrant Press and Its Control* (New York) 1922. *The City* (Chicago: Chicago Press) 1925, chap. 4.
7. Louis Wirth, *In The Ghetto* (Chicago: University of Chicago Press) 1928, refers to the press as an indicator of ethnic integrity, pp. 178–9, and as a factor in social integration, pp. 148, 162.
8. Cf. Breed, 'Social Control in the Newsroom', op. cit.

Bibliography

Aubert, V., *Sociology of Law* (London: Penguin) 1969.

Bacon, R. W., and Eltis, W. W., 'A Budget Message for Mr Healey: Get More People into Factories', *Sunday Times*, 10 Nov. 1974.

Baltzell, E. Digby, 'Who's Who in America' and 'The Social Register' in Bendix and Lipset, (1966), pp. 266–74.

Beauchamp, Murray, *Elements of Mathematical Sociology* (New York: Random House) 1970.

Becker, Howard S., *Outsiders: Studies in the Sociology of Deviance* (New York: Free Press) 1963.

Beith, A. J., 'The Councils and the Press', *New Society*, 9 Sept. 1965.

——, 'The Press and English Local Authorities', unpublished B.Litt. thesis, Nuffield College, Oxford, 1968.

Bendix, R., and Lipset, S. M. (eds.), *Class Status and Power* (London: Routledge & Kegan Paul) 1966.

Benet, James, 'Interpretation and Objectivity in Journalism', in Daniels and Kahn Hunt, 1970.

Berger, P., and Luckman T., *The Social Construction of Reality* (New York: Doubleday; London: Allen & Unwin) 1966.

Berkowitz, L., 'Film Violence and Subsequent Aggressive Tendencies', *Public Opinion Quarterly*, 27 (3), 1963, pp. 217–29.

Bernstein, Basil, *Class Codes and Control* (London: Routledge & Kegan Paul) 1972.

Bittner, E., 'The Concept of Organisation', in Turner (1974).

Blackburn, R., and Cockburn, A., *The Incompatibles* (London: Penguin) 1967.

Blau, Peter M., *The Dynamics of Bureaucracy* (Chicago: University of Chicago Press) 1955.

Blumberg, Abraham S., 'The Practice of Law as a Confidence Game', in Aubert (1969), pp. 321–31.

Boyd-Barret, Oliver, 'Journalism Recruitment and Training' in Tunstal, (1970), pp. 181–201.

Breed, Warren, 'Social Control in the Newsroom', *Social Forces*, No. 33, 1955, pp. 326–35.

Burns, T., 'Public Service and Private World', *Sociological Review Monographs*, ed. P. Halmos, Vol. 13, 1969, pp. 53–73.

Burns, T., and Stalker, G., *The Management of Innovation* (London: Tavistock) 1971.

Carter, R. E. (Jr), 'Newspaper Gatekeepers and the Sources of News', *Public Opinion Quarterly*, 22 (2), 1958, pp. 133–44.

Cicourel, Aaron V., *Method and Measurement in the Social Sciences* (New York: Free Press) 1964.

——, *The Social Organization of Juvenile Justice* (New York: Wiley) 1968.

Clements, Roger V., *Local Notables and the City Council* (London: Macmillan) 1969.

Crozier, M., *The Bureaucratic Phenomenon* (London: Tavistock) 1965.

Dahl, Robert A., *A Preface to Democratic Theory* (Chicago: University of Chicago Press) 1956.

——, *Who Governs?* (New Haven, Conn., N.J.: Yale University Press) 1961.

——, *Modern Political Analysis* (Englewood Cliffs, N.J.: Prentice-Hall) 1963.

Daniels, A. K., and Kahn Hunt, R. (eds.), *Academics on the Line* (San Francisco: Josey Bass) 1970.

Davison, W. Phillips, 'On the Effects of Communication' in Dexter and White (1964), pp. 68–89.

Deutsch, K. W., *Nationalism and Social Communication* (Cambridge, Mass.: Technological Press of M.I.T.) 1953.

——, *The Nerves of Government* (New York: Free Press) 1963.

Dexter, L. A., and White David, M. (eds.), *People, Society and Mass Communication* (New York: Free Press) 1964.

Donohew, Lewis, 'Newspaper Gatekeepers and Forces in the News Channel', *Public Opinion Quarterly*, 31 (1), 1967, pp. 61–9.

Durkheim, Emile, *The Division of Labor in Society* (New York: Free Press) 1964.

——, *Rules of Sociological Method* (New York: Free Press) 1964.

Elliott, P., 'Selection and Communication in Television Production' in Tunstall (1970), pp. 221–30.

——, *The Making of a Television Series* (London: Constable) 1972.

——, 'Mass Communication – A Contradiction in Terms' in McQuail (1972), pp. 237–58.

Finer, Samuel E., *Anonymous Empire: A Study of the Lobby in Great Britain* (London: Pall Mall) 1958.

Garfinkel, Harold, *Studies in Ethnomethodology* (Englewood Cliffs, N.J.: Prentice-Hall) 1968.

Gerbner, George, 'Mass Media and Human Communication Theory' in McQuail (1972), pp. 35–57.

Gerth, H. H., and Mills, C. Wright, (eds.), *From Max Weber* (London: Routledge & Kegan Paul) 1948.

Gieber, Walter, 'Across the Desk: A Study of 16 Telegraph Editors', *Journalism Quarterly*, 33, 1956, pp. 423–32.

——, 'News Is What Newspapermen Make It' in Dexter and White (1964), pp. 173–81.

Glazer, B., and Strauss, A. (eds.), *The Discovery of Grounded Theory* (London: Weidenfeld & Nicolson) 1967.

Glyn, Andrew, and Sutcliffe, Bob, *British Capitalism: Workers and the Profits Squeeze* (London: Penguin) 1972.

Goffman, Erving, *Interaction Ritual* (Chicago: Aldine) 1967.

Goldthorpe, R. and Lockwood, D., *The Affluent Worker: Industrial Attitudes and Behaviour* (Cambridge: Cambridge University Press) 1968.

Gouldner, A. V., *Patterns of Industrial Bureaucracy* (Chicago: Chicago University Press) 1955.

Hall, Stuart, 'Deviance, Politics and the Media' in Rock and McIntosh (1974), pp. 261–306.

Halloran, J. D., Elliott, P., and Murdock, G., *Demonstrations and Communications* (London: Penguin) 1972.

Hampton, W., *Democracy and Community, A Study of Politics in Sheffield* (London: Oxford University Press) 1970.

Hill, Dilys, 'Local Authorities and the Press', *Local Government Chronicle*, 11 Dec. 1965.

——, *Participating in Local Affairs* (London: Penguin) 1970.

Hunter, Floyd, *Community Power Structure* (Chapel Hill: University of North Carolina Press) 1963.

Hymans, Richard, *Strikes* (London: Penguin) 1972.

Jackson, Eric W., *Local Government in England and Wales* (London: Penguin) 1969.

Janowitz, Morris, *The Community Press in an Urban Setting* (Chicago: Chicago University Press) 1967.

Janowitz, M., and Berelson B. (eds.), *Public Opinion and Communication* (New York: Free Press) 1963.

Johnstone, J. W. C., Slavinski, E. J., and Bowman, W. B., 'The Professional Values of American Newsmen', *Public Opinion Quarterly*, Vol. 36, No. 4, 1972–3, pp. 522–40.

Judd, R., 'The Newspaper Reporter in a Suburban City', *Journalism Quarterly*, Vol. 38, Winter 1961, pp. 35–42.

Katz, D., and Kahn, R. L., *The Social Psychology of Organizations* (New York: John Wiley) 1967.

Kelmsley, *Manual of Journalism* (London:) 1954.

Kerr, C., and Siegel, A., 'Inter-Industry Propensity to Strike' in *Industrial Conflict*, ed. A. Kornhauser, Robert Dubin and Arthur M. Ross (New York: McGraw-Hill) 1954.

Key, V. O., *Public Opinion and American Democracy* (New York: Knopf) 1961.

Krupp, S., *Pattern and Organizational Analysis, A Critical Examination* (Philadelphia: Chilton) 1961.

Long, Norton E., 'The Local Community as an Ecology of Games', *American Journal of Sociology*, Vol. 64, Nov. 1958.

Lynd, Robert S., and Helen M., *Middletown in Transition* (New York: Harcourt Brace) 1957.

McHugh, Peter, *Defining the Situation* (New York: Bobbs Merrill) 1968.

McQuail, Denis, *Towards a Sociology of Mass Communication* (London: Collier-Macmillan) 1969.

McQuail, Denis, (ed.), *Sociology of Mass Communication* (London: Penguin) 1972.

McRae, T. W. (ed.), *Management Information Systems* (London: Penguin) 1971.

MacRorie, Ken, 'The Process of News Reporting', *Etc.*, Vol. 13, 1956, pp. 254–64.

Matejko, Aleksander, 'Newspaper Staff as a Social System' in Tunstall

(1970), pp. 168–80; reprinted from the *Polish Sociological Bulletin*, 1971, pp. 58–68.

Mannheim, Karl, *Ideology and Utopia* (London: Routledge & Kegan Paul) 1936.

Marshall, Sir Frank (chairman), '*The New Local Authorities*. Report of Study Group on Local Authority Management, Department of the Environment (London: HMSO) 1972.

Maud, Sir John (chairman), Ministry of Housing and Local Government Commission, Report on the Management of Local Government (London: HMSO) 1965.

Mayntz, R., 'The Study of Organisations', *Current Sociology*, 13, 1965.

Mayo, Elton, *The Social Problems of an Industrial Civilization* (Cambridge, Mass.: Harvard University Press) 1945.

Miliband, Ralph, *The State in Capitalist Society* (London: Quartet) 1973.

Miller, D. C., 'Decision Making Cliques in Community Power Structure', *American Journal of Sociology*, LXIV, Nov. 1958, pp. 299–310.

Mitchell, James Clyde (ed.), *Social Networks in Urban Situations* (Manchester: Manchester University Press) 1969.

Molotch, H., and Lester, M., 'News as Purposive Behavior', *American Sociological Review*, Vol. 39, No. 1, 1974, pp. 101–12.

Morris, D. S., and Newton K., 'Ominous Empires', unpublished paper, Birmingham University, 1971.

Mumford, Enid, 'Planning for Computers' in McRae (1971), pp. 317–30.

Murphy, David, 'The Unfreedom of the Local Press', *New Society*, 19 Dec. 1974.

Neustadt, I., *Presidential Power: The Politics of Leadership* (New York: John Wiley) 1961.

Newspaper Press Directory (London: Benn Brothers) annual publication.

Paletz, David L., Reichert, Peggy, and McIntyre, Barbara, 'How the Media Support Local Governmental Authority', *Public Opinion Quarterly*, Vol. XXXV, 1, Spring 1971, pp. 80–94.

Park, Robert E., *The Immigrant Press and Its Control* (New York:) 1922.

——, *The City* (Chicago: Chicago Press) 1925.

Parkin, Frank, *Middle Class Radicalism* (Manchester: Manchester University Press) 1968.

Polsby, N., *Community Power and Political Theory* (New Haven, Conn.: Yale University Press) 1963.

Pool, I. de Sola, 'Newsmen's Fantasies, Audiences and Newswriting', *Public Opinion Quarterly*, 23 (2), 1959, pp. 145–58; reprinted in Dexter and White (1964), pp. 141–59.

Pool, I. de Sola, and Schramm, W. (eds.), *Handbook of Communication* (Chicago: Rand McNally) 1973.

Redcliffe-Maud, Lord (chairman), Report of the Prime Minister's Committee on Local Government, Rules of Conduct, Cmnd 5636 (London: HMSO) 1974.

Richards, Peter G., *The New Local Government System* (London: Allen & Unwin) 1970.

Robson, William A., *Local Government in Crisis* (London: Allen & Unwin) 1966.

Rock, P., and McIntosh, M. (eds.), *Deviance and Social Control* (London: Tavistock) 1974.

Rose, Michael, *Computers, Managers and Society* (London: Penguin) 1969.

Royal Commission on the Press, 1947–1949, Report, Cmnd 7700, 1949.

Royal Commission on the Press, 1961, Report, Cmnd 1811, 1961.

Royal Commission on Local Government, Report Cmnd 4040, 1969.

Royko, Mike, *Boss: Mayor Richard J. Daly of Chicago* (London: Granada) 1972.

Schramm, Wilbur (ed.), *The Process and Effects of Mass Communication* (Urbana: University of Illinois Press) 1954.

Schumpeter, Joseph A., *Capitalism, Socialism and Democracy* (New York: Harper) 1942.

Sharrock, Wes, 'On Owning Knowledge' in Turner (1974).

Sigelman, L., 'Reporting the News, An Organizational Analysis', *American Journal of Sociology*, Vol. 79, 1973, pp. 132–51.

Smallwood, Frank, *Greater London, The Politics of Reform* (New York: Bobbs Merrill) 1965.

Spinrad, William, 'Power in Local Communities', *Social Problems*, Vol. 12, Winter 1965, pp. 335–56; reprinted in Bendix and Lipset (1966), pp. 218–30.

Stacey, Margaret, *Tradition and Change: A Study of Banbury* (London: Oxford University Press) 1960.

Strauss, A., *et al.*, *Psychiatric Ideologies and Institutions* (New York: Free Press) 1964.

Sykes, A. J. M., *et al.*, 'The Communist Connection', *The Observer*, 3 Feb. 1974.

Tuckman, Gaye, 'Making News by Doing Work: Routinizing the Unexpected', *American Journal of Sociology*, Vol. 79, No. 1, 1973, pp. 110–31.

Tunstall, Jeremy (ed.), *Media Sociology* (London: Constable) 1970.

Tunstall, Jeremy, *The Westminster Lobby Correspondents* (London: Routledge & Kegan Paul) 1970.

——, *Journalists at Work* (London: Constable) 1971.

——, 'News Organisation Goals and Specialist Newsgathering Journalists' in McQuail (1972), pp. 259–80.

Turner, Roy (ed.), *Ethnomethodology* (London: Penguin) 1974.

Warner, Lloyd, and Lunt, Paul S., *The Social Life of a Modern Community* (New Haven, Conn.: Yale University Press) 1941.

Warner, M., 'Decision Making in T.V. News', *Television Quarterly*, VII, 1968, pp. 60–75.

Weber, Max, *Economy and Society*, 3 Vols., ed. Guenther Rother and Claus Wittich (Totowa, N.J.: Bedminster) 1968.

White, David M., 'The Gatekeeper: A Case Study in the Selection of News', *Journalism Quarterly*, 27 (4), 1950, pp. 383–90; reprinted in Dexter and White (1964), pp. 160–73.

Wildavsky, A., *Leadership in a Small Town* (Totowa, N.J.: Bedminster) 1964.

Willis, J. Ramsay, Q.C., Report of the Bognor Regis Inquiry, Ministry of Housing and Local Government (London: HMSO) 1965.

Winch, Peter, *The Idea of a Social Science* (London: Routledge & Kegan Paul) 1958.

Wirth, Louis, *The Ghetto* (Chicago:) 1928.

Young, Jock, and Cohen, Stanley (eds.), *The Manufacture of News* (London: Constable) 1973.

Young, Jock, *Media as Myth* (London: Paladin) 1973.

——, 'Mass Media, Drugs and Deviance' in Rock and McIntosh (1974), pp. 229–60.

Zimmerman, D. H., 'Record-keeping and the Intake Process in a Public Welfare Organization' in *On Record: Files and Dossiers in American Life*, ed. Stanton Wheeler (Russell Sage Foundation) 1969.

Index